The Sovereign story

In 1988, Chris Coon and Ian Hendry set out to launch a new life insurance company in New Zealand. Most people thought they were mad. The industry was crowded with established companies, which in many cases had been around for several decades. Everyone knew that within the next 10 years there would be far fewer life companies as the big bought up the small. What chance would a new company have? These men had a crazy dream.

But Coon and Hendry, who had spent their working lives with successful life companies overseas, looked at the New Zealand market and saw only opportunities. They saw that the established life insurance companies were complacent and arrogant. These big companies seemed not to notice, or care about, the developments that had taken place overseas, and the New Zealand consumer was being offered inferior products as a result. Furthermore, the large companies were abusing the independent advisers who sold their products. They appeared to view them as a cost and a nuisance, not as customers who could make them successful. In Coon and Hendry's eyes, it was the reality of the New Zealand life insurance market that was crazy.

In January of 1989, with very little money and only a few staff, Sovereign opened for business. Twelve years later, the Sovereign group is one of New Zealand's largest financial services companies. Today, Sovereign has 34% of the country's life insurance business, which is twice as much as their nearest competitor. Two well-known established New Zealand life insurance companies, Metropolitan Life and Colonial, are now part of Sovereign. Sovereign has developed New Zealand's most successful system for administering investment funds, and the company is one of the top five investment companies in the country with over $3.5 billion under management. Sovereign is also the largest non-bank lender of mortgage funds in New Zealand.

Along the way, Coon and Hendry transformed the life industry in New Zealand. They introduced revolutionary new products and they set standards for service previously never seen in this country's life industry. They developed innovative ways of doing business, constantly improved them, and then re-invented them again. Coon and Hendry attracted talented people to work with them, gave them great opportunities to use those talents, and then looked after them so well that a great number are still with the company 12 years later. Indeed, the loyalty of Sovereign staff is legendary in the life industry.

Coon and Hendry have always understood that succeeding in business means taking risks, and they have never been afraid to launch new initiatives. Some, like their home mortgage business, were spectacularly successful. Others, such as New Zealand Superannuation Services, were failures. Coon and Hendry were always quick to build on their successes, and equally quick to acknowledge their mistakes, and fix them.

But most importantly, they never stopped being different.

Reality is Crazy

The remarkable story of Sovereign,
the company that revolutionised
the New Zealand life insurance industry.

by Ian Brooks
in association with Dwight Whitney

Published in 2001 Brooks on Business

An imprint of Nahanni Publishing Limited
PO Box 34-179, Birkenhead,
Auckland 1309, New Zealand
Tel. (09) 419 0681 Fax (09) 419 0695
info@nahanni-publishing.com

Copyright Ian Royston Brooks 2001

ISBN 09582036 4 4

All rights reserved. No part of this publication may be reproduced, stored in a retrieval system or transmitted in any form or by any means, electronic, mechanical, photocopying, recording or otherwise, without the prior written permission of the author.

Design and Production by Aviso Design Limited
Printed by Graphic Resources Limited

*It is not my dreams
that are crazy.
Reality is crazy.*

>Shimon Peres
>*Foreign Minister and
>former Prime Minister of Israel*

Table of Contents

INTRODUCTION		1
CHAPTER 1	The end of the beginning	7
CHAPTER 2	A room with a view	10
CHAPTER 3	The dream takes shape	14
CHAPTER 4	The first partner	20
CHAPTER 5	Piece by piece	27
CHAPTER 6	Hot products, hot service	39
CHAPTER 7	Have Yellow Pages will travel	46
CHAPTER 8	The backlash	56
CHAPTER 9	Business as usual	66
CHAPTER 10	One of our finest hours	79
CHAPTER 11	The revolution within	86
CHAPTER 12	The best laid schemes	91
CHAPTER 13	Meanwhile, sovereign re-invents itself	96
CHAPTER 14	Building the brand	125
CHAPTER 15	The MetLife purchase: one giant step forward	136
CHAPTER 16	Home mortgages: another great success	144
CHAPTER 17	New Zealand Superannuation Services: one small step back	148
CHAPTER 18	Going public at last	154
CHAPTER 19	A new beginning	157
CHAPTER 20	We're back	162
CHAPTER 21	The Colonial merger: another great leap forward	167
CHAPTER 22	The challenge ahead	174
EPILOGUE	What you can learn from the Sovereign story	179
	About the authors	189
ILLUSTRATIONS	Photographs of Sovereign's people and events over the years	105

The earliest known photo of Sovereign's management team. This is reproduced from a polaroid, thought to have been taken in 1989. From left to right: Don Jefferies, Chris Coon, Ian Hendry, David Whyte and Naomi Ballantyne.

Introduction

I first met Chris Coon in the early 1990s when I went to collect my son from Coon's house one Saturday afternoon. Our sons were schoolmates and they had spent the day together. Since I had not met Coon before, we spent a few minutes chatting on the doorstep. With his lithe body and youthful face, he looks much younger than his years. His large glasses and an equally large smile dominate his face. He is softly spoken and a man of few words, especially about himself. But his insights are very perceptive and his comments can be cutting. At such times his eyes twinkle mischievously and an impish smile crosses his face. He is very much a gentleman but, like Hendry, underneath there is a toughness. Coon knows what he wants, and once he sets his mind on a goal it would be a foolhardy person who stood in his way. But I had yet to learn these things. In the little time we had together on that Saturday, I only managed to establish that Coon was from England and had been in New Zealand just a few years. An immigrant to New Zealand myself, I was interested in why he had come out here to live. In characteristic understatement Coon replied, "I came to start an insurance company," and that was the end of the conversation. At that point Sovereign had a staff of 40 and its sales were $12 million per year.

I next encountered Coon and Hendry in 1996 when Daryl McAlinden, the managing director of Caledonian Financial Services, invited me to sit on the company's board. Although Caledonian was 100% owned by Sovereign, McAlinden and Hendry had decided that the board would benefit from appointing two outside directors. For two and a half years, I participated in monthly board meetings with Hendry and Coon, and during this time Sovereign purchased MetLife and went through the New Zealand Superannuation Services fiasco. This gave me a wonderful opportunity to see how Coon and Hendry thought and behaved when they were under pressure. Even then they were full of dreams, but what was more impressive was the way they handled things when some of their dreams turned to custard.

My associate, Dwight Whitney, has an even longer association with Sovereign. He and his partner Kaye Coyne were one of the first suppliers Coon and Hendry engaged. As Sovereign's marketing consultants from 1988 to the end of 1999, they guided the development of the Sovereign brand, the company launch, and numerous product launches and advertising campaigns.

Dwight and I encouraged Coon and Hendry to document Sovereign's history because it is one of the best business stories in New Zealand's history. Coon and Hendry each looked at a crowded and competitive marketplace, as the insurance industry was in the 1980s, and unlike everyone else saw only opportunities. Moreover, they had the courage to abandon their very successful careers and risk all of their assets to turn their dream into reality. Most importantly though, by following some very good basic business principles, they steered Sovereign through a decade of chaos, as the financial services industry in New Zealand re-invented itself. They transformed Sovereign from being just a handwritten business plan into a major financial services company. Along the way, Coon and Hendry became millionaires.

At first their competitors considered them a joke. Then, as Sovereign began to win new business and gain market share, they took the new kids on the block seriously and retaliated. Regretfully, the battle was fought not only in the market place with better products and improved service, but in back rooms with gossip, rumour and personal attacks. Even government agencies such as the Securities Commission, became involved in the battle to defeat the upstarts. This is the story of how a few brave people refused to be intimidated by the established life companies bent on destroying them, and government bureaucrats long on prejudice and short on expertise. It took years of work and millions of dollars to convince New Zealand regulators that what Sovereign was doing was not alchemy but simply good business practice commonly found overseas. Sovereign is the story of how a few visionary people, convinced there was a better way and passionate about their cause, would change forever the way the life insurance industry operated in this country. They would also influence industry practice in Australia.

Even today, when Sovereign is writing more business than any other company in New Zealand, there are many who dismiss what the Englishman and the Scotsman have accomplished as having been simply the result of good luck: "They were in the right place at the right time," say the cynics. "They were lucky to hire good people. They were lucky to have the backing of good reassurers and fund managers." The doubters will say, "Sovereign is the largest life company in the country only because its parent company acquired Colonial in Australia." But the Sovereign story is living proof of the adage: "The harder I work, the luckier I get."

The fairy tale story of Sovereign contains many lessons for business leaders entering the 21st century, the era of the entrepreneur. Today, more than ever, people are leaving (either willingly or unwillingly) their positions in large corporations or government departments to become self-employed. Many others, who made the move several years ago, are now striving to grow their small businesses into larger ones. In this environment, the question on every entrepreneur's mind is, "how do you succeed in business?"

The first lesson the Sovereign story teaches is never underestimate the power of an entrepreneur's dream. Each of today's successful businesses once existed only in the minds of an entrepreneur who had an idea that they believed would succeed, although most others believed it would not. As the Sovereign story shows, the dream starts with someone spotting an opportunity that no one else has seen. I once read that each of us comes across more opportunities in a day than we could possibly develop in a lifetime, but few of us see them. Like the artist or the inventor, the entrepreneur sees what the rest of us cannot see. That is their gift. But after they have developed the opportunity and it is visible to all, we say, "Of course that was a good idea. He was just lucky to be in the right place at the right time."

A dream by itself, of course, is worthless. The successful entrepreneur must act. Entrepreneurs are people who understand that business is a four-letter word spelled R I S K. Paradoxically, entrepreneurs do not so much have courage as they have faith. It just never occurs to them that they will fail. This is not an arrogance about their own ability; rather it is a belief, often a naive belief, in the soundness of their idea. As Ian Hendry said three years after Sovereign opened its doors, "If we'd known four years ago what we know now, we wouldn't have done it." But they persevered and ironically many of the 'established' companies which dominated the marketplace when Sovereign was just a dream, which predicted with confidence that Sovereign would fold within two years of opening its doors, and which worked hard to make that prediction come true, today have either disappeared or are struggling to survive.

The Sovereign story is an object lesson showing that wealth is created for owners and employees only because value has first been created for customers. It is a story showing how investment in people, innovation and technology pays huge dividends. It is a story illustrating the benefits of constant improvement, and showing there is always a better way, you just have to find it. For 25 years I have been associated with successful business people all over the world, and the one thing I have

learned is that the recipe for success is always the same:
1. Put your customers first;
2. Operate efficient processes;
3. Develop your people into teams;
4. Re-invent your business.

The Sovereign story is proof this recipe works.

Sovereign's founders, Chris Coon and Ian Hendry, would be the first to admit that they were not always aware they were following such a recipe. Like most entrepreneurs, they operated by intuition. At Sovereign, they even had a name for it: They called it golden guts. "The fact is, we have done most of the things we should have done," says Ian Hendry, who retires this year as managing director of the Sovereign Group. "We just didn't recognise what we were doing. We have blundered from pillar to post, but fortunately most of our blundering has really been quite successful. A lot of what we have done has turned out to be the right things without us knowing they were the right things." But Hendry is being modest. As you learn about the Sovereign story, you will see these four principles are the basis of its success.

Coon and Hendry began their journey to success by seeing the opportunity to create superior value for both independent advisers and policyholders alike. Unlike their competitors, Coon and Hendry considered the independent advisers to be Sovereign's key customers, and therefore just as important as the policyholders. They believed that if they created superior value for these two customer groups, they would succeed. They rarely lost sight of that objective. Later, along with key senior managers such as Naomi Ballantyne, Richard Coon, and David Anderson, Coon and Hendry focused on improving the efficiency and effectiveness of Sovereign's business processes, and on developing a customer driven culture, knowing this would both improve customer retention and reduce costs at the same time. Coon and Hendry also made investing in people a top priority. They hired those they believed were the best, provided inspired leadership and looked after them well. Finally, and perhaps most importantly, Sovereign's people worked constantly to re-invent their business. At no time did they relax and become complacent. There was always another challenge to conquer before they would be satisfied.

The Sovereign story is not just educational; it is inspirational. This is a story of personal courage, perseverance and triumph, showing that even in a complex, chaotic, highly competitive global market place, two men with brilliance, conviction and determination can build a major company from nothing. It is also a story of business triumph, in the tradition of Richard and Ken Carter, James Fletcher, Stephen Tindall and Douglas Myers, illustrating that business owners can create wealth for themselves and at the same time create wealth for their fellow shareholders, for their customers and for their staff. And, that you do not have to compromise your principles to succeed.

I am indebted to Chris Coon and Ian Hendry for making themselves, their people and their records available to me. I am also grateful to Dwight Whitney for carrying out much of the research into Sovereign's history and for helping me understand all that has transpired over the past 12 years. It should be made clear, however, that although others helped me tell this story, the conclusions reached are mine alone and I take full responsibility for what is written.

Ian Brooks
Auckland,
October, 2001

"If we'd known four years ago what we know now, we wouldn't have done it."

Ian Hendry, 1992

"I wouldn't have changed it for the world. The last few years have been fantastic."

Ian Hendry, 2001

"I hadn't realised until today just how much risk we had taken."

Chris Coon, 1992

"I have absolutely no regrets. It has been a wonderful ride."

Chris Coon, 2001

CHAPTER 1

The end of the beginning

"You wouldn't be human if you could not take satisfaction from taking a concept and turning it into the largest life insurance company in New Zealand, especially when no one gave you a chance."

It is a sunny clear crisp July morning. From the glass wall at the far end of the 3rd floor executive office, you can see the sun sparkling on the turquoise waters of the Hauraki Gulf. The bush-clad cone of Rangitoto sits up so clearly you think you can reach out the window and touch it. Ian Hendry sits back in the plush leather lounge suite looking more relaxed than I have seen him look for years. In fact, just a few minutes earlier I heard him singing in the corridor. The man who co-founded Sovereign Assurance, arguably one of New Zealand's most successful companies, has recently made the decision to retire at the end of this year, although it will not be public knowledge for a couple of months yet. He needs to keep it quiet until ASB Bank, Sovereign's owners since 1998, has found someone to replace him. In the next-door office, which is equally spacious and also has a spectacular view of the Gulf, Chris Coon, the actuary who in the mid 1980s could see what no one else could see, works at his computer, generating new financial models or tweaking old ones. In a few weeks, he too will announce his retirement, although in Coon's case he says he will continue to consult to Sovereign. It will surprise no one when he makes the announcement. Coon without Hendry is like Nureyev without Fontaine, or Rodgers without Hammerstein.

"So, after 13 years you have made the big decision?" I ask Hendry. He stretches his arm expansively across the back of the chair and his face breaks into a broad grin. His blue-grey eyes twinkle. "It is time to go," he says, his Scottish brogue little affected by 20 years as an expatriate. "I made the decision some time ago. When ASB acquired us, I agreed to a two-year contract, so 2000 would have been a natural jumping-off place. But I couldn't go then because of the Colonial merger. I said I would stay until that was completed which it now is." It was an easy decision to make, Hendry tells me. "The company needs a different sort of manager now. I am a better builder than maintainer of a company. My satisfaction comes from taking something new and making it work from scratch. Today Sovereign needs a corporate animal because we are a very substantial company."

One of the first things you notice about Hendry is his friendly face, topped by the snow-white hair, brushed back like a mane. His manner is easy-going, and you never get far into the conversation before his booming laughter fills the room. He expresses his thoughts well, and with a large repertoire of stories, a quick wit and a ready sense of humour, he is entertaining to listen to. Between the down-to-earth relaxed way he has with people, and the comfortable lounge furniture that fills one corner of his large office, you feel like a guest in his house rather than an employee meeting with the chief executive. It is easy to see how he has been able to capture the hearts and minds of his staff, and to hold their loyalty over the years. Underneath the genuine warmth is a man with a thick skin and the toughness to make very difficult decisions. "Oh, I am no delicate flower," he laughs when I suggest he is being defensive.

Over coffee and chocolate biscuits, we discuss the changes that have taken place in the past few years. Sovereign acquired MetLife and doubled in size in one fell swoop in 1996. Sovereign tried to list on the stock exchange twice and when it finally succeeded in 1998, it was a fizzle. In spite of this, the company continued to write more new business than any other life company in New Zealand. In 1996, Sovereign entered the mortgage market and today is the largest non-bank lender in the country. In 1998, they launched Aegis, which is the largest investment wrap account in New Zealand. Caledonian Financial Services, Sovereign's wholly owned 'independent' brokerage, has gone but Sovereign has created the SovNet from CFS and the tied agency force it acquired with the MetLife purchase. Successful Money Management Seminars has been sold back to Laura and Okke Hansen who were among the very first brokers to sell Sovereign products. It has profited from acquiring and then selling companies such as S H Lock, Reeves Moses and Metlifecare. Sovereign, a company barely 13 years old has absorbed Colonial, a brand that has been in New Zealand for more than 100 years.

On the people side, Naomi Ballantyne, the first manager to be employed by Coon and Hendry in 1988 has left to start her own insurance company. Ernie Uganecz, the first person to buy into Coon and Hendry's dream, has gone with her. David Whyte, another early key employee, is general manager of a competing life company. Dennis Ferrier and Bruce Bornholdt, Sovereign's first two chairmen have passed away. Some of the independent brokers in the industry who saw Sovereign as their white knight have been through several mergers in the past few years and have become cynical and wary of Sovereign. Many are having trouble coming to terms with Sovereign's integration of Colonial in particular. On the upside, "business today is fantastic," Hendry tells me with pride. "Sovereign's total business is now greater than the combined business of Colonial and Sovereign 12 months ago."

We continue to reflect on the past. Sometimes Hendry shows his pride at what he and Coon have accomplished, sometimes the old passion and excitement with which he built Sovereign comes through, and sometimes he remembers with sadness. Hendry was particularly close to Bruce Bornholdt, a barrister who became Sovereign's second chairman. They worked very closely together in the early days when Sovereign was on the brink of being closed by New Zealand's regulators, and he feels Bornholdt's recent death keenly. "Do you have any regrets, Ian?" I ask him, knowing full well what the answer will be. "I wouldn't have changed it for the world," he says emphatically. "The last few years have been fantastic. I have had the opportunity to take a concept, create a structure on paper, and then turn it into a living, breathing organisation. I have really enjoyed seeing people grow and develop. That has given me great satisfaction. You wouldn't be human if you could not take satisfaction from taking a concept and turning it into the largest life insurance company in New Zealand, especially when no one gave you a chance."

"The last few years have been fantastic. I have had the opportunity to take a concept, create a structure on paper, and then turn it into a living, breathing organisation."

CHAPTER 2

A room with a view

"Everyone thought I was insane giving up a well-paid safe job and going to the other side of the world with four small children."

Every successful company begins with a dream, and in Sovereign's case the dream belonged to Chris Coon. Coon was one of the few people in New Zealand to be bullish about business after the share market crash of 1987. For most New Zealanders that was a time for retrenchment, but in a cramped attic bedroom in Auckland's North Shore, Coon sat at his 286 computer grinding out financial models, convinced that before him lay the opportunity to start a new life insurance company. He was without doubt the only person in New Zealand to believe that. At that time, the accepted view was that there were already far too many insurance companies fighting for too little business. In the mid eighties, 80% of the total annual life business in New Zealand was written by the five largest companies, leaving little premium income to share among the 20 smaller companies. According to industry experts, the prospects for existing companies were bleak, and for a new life company they were disastrous. "Like banking, the insurance industry in New Zealand is heading for quite a shake-up within the next couple of years," begins an article in the June 25th 1987 edition of *The New Zealand Herald*. The article went on to predict there would be continued rationalisation within the industry with only 15 of the 37 companies surviving. But such views did not diminish Coon's confidence. A quiet man with a very keen and analytical mind, especially where numbers are concerned, Coon was optimistic: "I tend not to see the world in the same way as others do," he says with a twinkle in his eyes.

Long before the 1987 crash Coon had decided that New Zealand offered a unique opportunity to launch a new life assurance company, and he had a good vantage point from which to view the industry. Firstly, as an outsider he was not bound by the traditions and paradigms of the New Zealand life industry. Secondly, he was a very talented actuary with many years experience in the life assurance business in both Europe and North America.

Coon was born and raised in England but because his wife, Yvonne, is a New Zealander he had made numerous visits to New Zealand over the years. On each trip he made a point of meeting with the dozen or so actuaries working in life offices and this gave him a clear picture of how the industry was developing. Coon believed the industry was mired in tradition and that the established companies were arrogant and conservative and this convinced him that a new life company with a very different approach would succeed. "I had a very good idea of the market," he says, "and I could see that it was really very inefficient, with very poor products. Most of the life offices had tied agencies and they treated both their agents and the independent brokers very poorly." Coon also saw that New Zealand life offices were ignoring the developments in the insurance industry overseas. Indeed, in spite of the industry being deregulated in this country, New Zealand companies appeared to deny their own market was changing. "They seemed determined to do in the future those things that had worked for them in the past," says Coon. "They were unable or unwilling to see that the industry was changing." All of this gave Coon encouragement because he knew that their complacency and tunnel vision provided him with a business opportunity.

When Coon looked at the New Zealand life industry, he did so with experienced and skilled eyes. After graduating from Nottingham University with a degree in mathematics, he began his career in the life insurance industry in Britain with Guardian. Two years later, he went to New York to work for New York Life, but to avoid being drafted to Vietnam, he returned to London and joined Bacon & Woodrow, one of Britain's leading consulting actuaries, and soon became a partner. After five years, Coon went to Abbey Life, a company most UK actuaries tried to work for during some part of their careers. After a short stint with Abbey Life, Coon moved to Fidelity Life. This, too, was a short stay. Fidelity got into financial difficulties as a result of the secondary banking collapse in the UK in 1974. Coon insisted the shareholders put more capital into the company to protect the policyholders and when the shareholders did not agree, he left.

Coon moved to Liberty Life, which had also been hit hard by the banking collapse in 1974. Liberty's directors had courted him for a number of months but Coon refused to join the company unless the directors injected more capital into the company, so that the policyholders had more protection. In the middle of 1975 they did, and Coon joined the firm as a senior manager and company actuary. Over the next few years, he became increasingly dissatisfied with Liberty, however. "There were a number of problems in the company that made making a profit quite difficult," says Coon dryly. "Sales people were writing poor quality business which did not stay on the books very long." Liberty was by no means unique in this regard. During the 1970s and 1980s, many British life companies were having difficulty adjusting to the threats of greater deregulation and increased competition, and were writing low quality business as a result. Concerned about this trend, Coon decided he would go out on his own. "I saw the future for a low quality life assurance company as becoming increasingly difficult," he says and events would prove him right. Liberty Life later disappeared in a company take-over.

Coon's time at Liberty persuaded him that he could run a very successful life company based on writing good quality business. Moreover, during his years in the industry, Coon had developed an excellent reputation among senior people in some of the foremost re-insurance companies in the world, and he was confident that if he ever did start his own company, he would have their support. He was right, and this support was later to be a critical factor in Sovereign's survival.

"New Zealand was the only country in the western world where it would have been possible to start a new company without a large amount of money."

Dissatisfied with Liberty, and with the dream of starting his own life insurance company firmly planted in his mind, Coon began looking seriously at moving to New Zealand. "When I first started coming to New Zealand," he recalls, "I looked at the life insurance industry and at that time it was heavily regulated. There was just no way one could introduce the kind of products that I'd spent most of my life developing. But by 1982, de-regulation was beginning and I realised that everything I had worked on in the UK was now directly applicable to New Zealand." Coon also recognised that New Zealand laws made starting a new life company relatively easy. "New Zealand was the only country in the western world where it would have been possible to start a new company without a large amount of money," he says. It also appeared that once a life company was set up it would be able to operate quite freely. Although the New Zealand Justice Department monitored life companies, direct government control of the industry was minimal. The directors of Sovereign would later discover, to their considerable personal and financial cost, they had underestimated the interest regulatory agencies would take in their new venture.

Convinced there was an opportunity for him to develop his dream in New Zealand, Coon made his move. "On one holiday in 1984, I decided that we were going to move down here and set up a life company. I went back to England and set about to do that," he recalls. For her part, Yvonne Coon was happy about returning to New Zealand. How did she feel about risking everything they owned to start a new life company? "She had total confidence in me," Coon says laughing, "and probably like me, wasn't aware of all the dangers involved."

The Coon family left the U.K. at the end of 1986, six weeks after child number four was born. "Everyone thought I was insane giving up a well paid safe job and going to the other side of the world with four small children," says Coon grinning. The first priority was to put food on the table and to do that he accepted a number of actuarial consulting assignments. Because of his strong ethics, he took care to avoid a conflict of interests and he always declared that his intent was to establish his own life company. "Everyone thought it was a big joke," he recalls. "And because they didn't take me seriously, a number of companies approached me to join them full-time."

Much of Coon's consulting work was with the Justice Department investigating both life offices, and fire and general insurance companies. These assignments not only provided an income, they gave him yet another opportunity to study the New Zealand life companies that would be his future competition. This experience confirmed his earlier impressions that many were operating poorly. "I found that there were a number of companies which were not so much dishonest but incompetent," says Coon. "Their records were so poor that it was very hard to get proper information. I would get what hard numbers I could, and then use them to paint a picture of the problems they were facing." Convinced he would be competing against fat, old fashioned companies which were unwilling to change, led by managers who were still living in Fortress New Zealand, seemingly unconcerned about what was happening elsewhere in the world, Coon decided it was the reality of the New Zealand life industry, not his dreams, that were crazy. With renewed confidence, he set about turning his dream into reality.

He would transform the life industry in New Zealand in the process.

CHAPTER 3

The dream takes shape

"I recognised that here was an amazing chance to shake up the life assurance establishment which had become lazy and complacent, and was doing nothing to provide performance and value for its policy holders."

When he was not consulting, Coon could be found in his small attic study with its magnificent view of the Hauraki Gulf, doing the things he loved doing best. He wrote computer programs, built intricate financial models and developed business plans showing how his new life company would develop. He outlined the products he planned to sell, described the anticipated market conditions, and forecast the expected sales. During this time of planning, Coon also secured the capital he would need by raising money against his own assets, and by persuading friends and family to invest in his new venture. In these days of planning and preparation, Coon also networked with brokers, especially larger broker organisations, letting them know about his intention to launch a new life company. But most importantly, he tried to find the people he would need to turn this dream into reality by sharing his vision with whomever would listen.

As with everything he does, Coon's business plans for the new company were thorough. His early files contain pages of painstakingly detailed notes written in small neat handwriting. "The following business plan," one sheaf of notes begins, "shows a strain over the first two years operation of $813,000. A further $500,000 is required to be placed with the Public Trustee. Surplus would emerge in Year 3. Thus issued capital of $2,000,000 would be required, allowing for some deviation from the business plan." Coon had been able to raise one million dollars himself ("Yvonne and I mortgaged ourselves to the hilt," he says) and he set out to get the rest by convincing others about the potential of his dream. Because of his passion and his meticulous planning, this turned out to be very easy and Coon was able to raise the second million dollars from business associates and family members who invested anywhere from $20,000 to $50,000 each. Coon's business plan contained fourteen more pages of tightly hand-scripted pages describing the products, outlining budgets and showing very detailed actuarial calculations. He also outlined the people he would need as the business grew. Coon believed he would need a marketing person, someone with administrative skills, an IT operator and an accountant. "I thought we needed to start the operation with about ten people building to about 50 over four or five years. I had hoped we wouldn't need any more than that!" he says grinning. In 2001, Sovereign had over 800 employees with major offices in Auckland and Wellington.

Coon's approach to product development was to begin with the products and services that were being marketed in Britain at that time. He then spent two years studying the New Zealand market conditions and adapting the UK products to the local market. One of the lessons Coon had learned from Liberty was to avoid poor quality business. Therefore, right from the beginning, his aim was to provide brokers with quality products that would attract long-term customers. He then encouraged them to seek the right kind of sales by building a commission structure into the products that very aggressively rewarded brokers who wrote business that stayed on the books. "We also put measurements in place," says Coon, "so that we could identify brokers who were writing poor persistency business (signing up people who terminated their policies quickly) and weed them out."

As any entrepreneur knows, coming up with the great business idea is often easy compared to the challenge of securing adequate start-up funding. In Coon's case, however, raising start-up capital was only part of the challenge in funding his new business because insurance companies have a unique funding problem and are very capital intensive. Any start-up business requires seed capital to establish a place of business, purchase equipment, hire staff and develop marketing material. In the early days money goes out with nothing coming back, but then the orders start to roll in and with money flowing in instead of just out, the future looks rosier. But it is not that simple for life insurance companies because every sale costs them far more than they earn from the sale. All of the first year's premium, and sometimes more, is paid as commission to the

The problem for new life companies is that the more successful they are in selling new policies, the more money they lose.

broker making the sale. In addition to paying the broker, the life company has the costs of administering the new policy. This involves underwriters and clerical staff processing the application, accepting the risk and issuing the policy documents. It is usually only in the third year of a policy's life that the company starts to earn a surplus; that is to say, to receive more from the annual premium than it costs to sell and service the policy. The problem for new life companies, then, is that the more successful they are in selling new policies, the more money they lose. People in the life industry in New Zealand understood this, of course, and that is why they did not believe that Sovereign could survive more than a few months, or a couple of years at the most. They knew that Sovereign was beginning with relatively little capital and were convinced the company could not withstand the losses associated with winning and processing new business. The more successful Sovereign was in making sales, the more certain they were it would go under. It was for this reason that in the early days many independent advisers refused to recommend Sovereign's products to their clients.

But not only was Sovereign able to survive its initial marketing success, it flourished. This was due to an arrangement Coon had negotiated with two of the world's top reassurance companies. Reassurance companies play an important role in the insurance industry. When people buy insurance, they are buying security and protection against risk. But insurance companies must protect themselves too. A big disaster such as the recent terrorist attacks in the United States could cause a company to have underwriting losses so large as to threaten its very existence. Therefore insurance companies spread their risk by reinsuring with companies that specialise in this type of insurance. In 1988, it was common for life companies in New Zealand to use reassurance companies to protect them from large losses and nothing more. But Coon knew that the reassurance companies could not only share his risk, they could solve his problem of how to fund a rapidly expanding business. This arrangement was not a radical concept. Indeed it was common practice in Europe but it was unknown in New Zealand and Australia. "There was nothing terribly complicated about the ideas," says Coon. "They were being used quite extensively from the late 1960s onwards, and I was quite surprised that actuaries in New Zealand didn't grasp what we were doing."

In essence, the reassurers became partners in Sovereign's business.

When a new policy was written, not only did the reassurers accept 95% of the risk thereby reducing the reserve Sovereign would have to set aside against future claims, but they also advanced the company an amount of money nearly twice the annual premium. This paid for the costs of administering the new policy and removed the major financial strain of writing new business. As a result, this arrangement allowed Sovereign to pursue new business aggressively. It was a classic win-win situation for both Sovereign and their re-insurance companies. Not only did Sovereign get the funding it needed, the reassurers secured a flow of first class business and an attractive return on the money advanced. By the time Sovereign was purchased by the ASB Bank in 1999, the reassurers had advanced Sovereign approximately NZ$100 million through this arrangement.

Coon was able to negotiate this partnership arrangement with Cologne Re, and Gerling Globale, two of Europe's leading reassurers, because of the respect he had earned with the top managers of these companies. They had been so impressed with Coon's performance at Liberty Life that they had indicated early on that they were keen to be involved in his new venture. Few others in the life industry could have gained such support, and the involvement of senior people who were leaders of very reputable global companies made it easier for Coon to attract other investors, people who might otherwise have been nervous about putting their money into a start-up life company. "After all, it is easy to lose your shirt in this business," Coon says wryly. This partnership with some of the world's biggest re-insurance companies not only made the new company financially viable, it later saved Sovereign from a threat Coon would never have imagined, even in his worst nightmares.

The two principal foundations of Coon's business plan, then, were to offer a different type of insurance product and the partnership he had developed with two of the world's largest reassurers. Neither of these was unique by international standards, but they had been ignored in New Zealand as a result of the arrogance or complacency of the players in the New Zealand market. Being large organisations with strong international connections these companies must have known what was happening overseas both in new product development and re-insurance. Did they believe that the New Zealand consumer did not deserve better insurance products? Could they not be bothered trying to understand how Sovereign might structure its business so it could survive a period of rapid growth in new business? Or, was it simply that it suited them not to understand so they could sow seeds of doubt in the industry and accomplish in the back rooms what they could not do in the market place? "I find it quite remarkable,' says Coon with ill-concealed contempt, "that they had such a poor understanding of what we were doing, bearing in mind that the products they were offering here were so far behind what was being sold in the U.K. and that their own companies in England were using these new products. There seems to have been no sharing of ideas from the U.K. companies to their subsidiaries here."

With business plans in place, with products developed (at least conceptually), and with funding secured, Coon set out to take the next step in turning his dream into reality. One of the characteristics of successful people is that they know both their strengths and their weaknesses. Coon knew he had the skills and experience to manage the financial side of a life insurance company. More importantly, he knew that he had both the vision and the passion to make his new venture work. But he also knew he could never run a company on a day-to-day basis. "Managing people, developing marketing programs and implementing administrative systems is not my forte," he admits with a smile. "I have no skills in administration and absolutely no interest in it." Most importantly, Coon realized that even if he had these skills, he could not perform what was required on the financial front and do much else, so from the moment he got the idea to start an insurance company, he started looking for a partner to develop the business. "It never entered my mind to look for an employee," he says. "I knew it had to be someone to build the company with me."

> *Coon's most critical task before opening for business was to find someone who had the operational skills and marketing knowledge that he lacked.*

Coon's most critical task before opening for business was to find someone who had the operational skills and marketing knowledge that he lacked. This person needed to have had considerable experience running a life company, and they had to understand what was happening in the industry overseas, not just in New Zealand and Australia. It was essential that this individual shared Coon's vision and excitement about what could be accomplished in New Zealand. They had to have the courage to risk everything in a venture the experts predicted would fail, and the stamina to persevere no matter what obstacles were placed in their path. But most importantly, this person had to be someone Coon could get on with and could trust, for theirs would be a long-term partnership that would take them through some very rough terrain.

He found him in Hong Kong.

CHAPTER 4

The first partner

"The man had vision. He had a clear idea of what he wanted to achieve. He was a person who had incredible enthusiasm and who could see nothing to prevent him from achieving his goals."

Ian Hendry, a Scotsman working in Hong Kong for a British life company, became the first person to share Coon's dream. Hendry took an instant liking to Coon when they first met in 1988. "Chris is impossible to dislike," he says, "even when he does things that drive you round the bend." Like others who had heard Coon talk about his dream, Hendry was inspired by Coon's passion and his determination. "The man had vision. He had a clear idea of what he wanted to achieve. He was a person who had incredible enthusiasm and who could see nothing to prevent him from achieving his goals." But most of all Hendry was excited by the rare opportunity to run his own insurance company and to shake up the life industry. "I was very attracted to what Chris was doing in New Zealand. I recognised that here was an amazing chance to shake up the life assurance establishment which had become lazy and complacent, and was doing nothing to provide performance and value for its policyholders."

Coon heard about Hendry from Duncan Ferguson, Hendry's boss at Eagle Star. Coon had realised from the outset that if his new life company was to succeed, it had to have credibility, and he believed this could best be achieved by being associated with a large established international life company such as Eagle Star. Consequently he met with Ferguson, a man he had known for many years, outlined his plans for starting a new company in New Zealand and suggested Eagle Star invest in the new venture. He also told Ferguson that he was looking for a partner who had experience in the day-to-day operations of a life company. Ferguson was excited by Coon's plans and keen to see Eagle Star involved in the new company. He also recommended Coon talk to Hendry who, in his opinion, had the skills and experience Coon was looking for. While these discussions about his future were taking place, Hendry was leading the good life in Hong Kong where he was happily running Eagle Star's Asian office. He had never heard of Coon and he was blissfully unaware of his boss's suggestion that he move several thousand miles and set up a new life company in New Zealand.

Hendry was already a long way from home. Born in Glasgow, he chose to work in the insurance industry after high school only because he was not successful in getting the job he really wanted. "I always wanted to become a journalist," he says, "so in secondary school, to the headmaster's horror, I opted to take courses such as shorthand and typing which meant I had to drop a couple of more academic subjects. It also meant I was the only boy in an entire class of girls in those subjects!" Hendry had his heart set on working for the *Glasgow Herald* and when he finished high school a position became vacant. He applied, and so did 400 others. Hendry made the short-list of four but did not get the job. He decided to join the insurance industry because, like banking, it was considered to be a safe career. "If you worked 50 years and didn't do anything awful, they gave you a nice pension at the end," he says with a chuckle. His first job was with Scottish Mutual doing clerical work and he immediately set out to improve his fortunes by taking industry courses, becoming one of the youngest people ever to complete the Chartered Insurance Institute examination course. After four years' experience with head office administrative procedures, it was suggested that Hendry move into sales and he readily agreed. "I said that sounds all right. You get a motor car and you are reasonably well paid if you are successful, so when can I start?" They told him he could begin when he was 25. The problem for Hendry was that he was only 20 at the time.

Deciding that he could short-circuit the system by moving elsewhere, Hendry joined the brokerage firm of Turner & Copeland as the assistant to the life and pensions manager. There were only the two of them in the department and the manager spent most of his time

"I was assistant to the manager but I often forgot to include the word 'to' in my title so I became a life and pensions manager fairly quickly."

involved in Conservative Party politics. "I was assistant to the manager but I often forgot to include the word *to* in my title so I became a life and pensions manager fairly quickly," he grins. During that time, he met a broker development manager from Eagle Star who told him he was leaving his job to become a full-time lecturer in life insurance education. Hendry successfully applied for his job and within two years he had been voted Life Salesman of the Year. Four years later, he was moved to London to manage the West End life office.

Fourteen years after joining Eagle Star, Hendry was posted to Hong Kong as Life Agency manager for the company's new Far Eastern agency operation and twelve months later he became general manager of that division. For six years, Hendry grew Eagle Star's business in the Far East. He loved his time in Hong Kong, both the business challenges and the lifestyle. A keen and competitive player of lawn bowls, he had ample opportunity to develop his skills in spite of working long hours. Indeed, Hendry would have happily remained in Hong Kong but his wife, June, was ready to leave. "She could see more clearly than I, the trap you could fall into in living in Hong Kong," he admits. "It is a very privileged lifestyle and it is easy to get hooked into having servants, club memberships and a high income. June decided she wanted to live a more normal life and wanted to put down some roots somewhere and settle down. This didn't particularly appeal to me. I was quite happy being unsettled and having a good time!"

June prevailed and Hendry reviewed his options. None of them were very appealing. Eagle Star's parent company, British American Tobacco, had just acquired a company in America called The Farmers Group and Eagle Star had earmarked Hendry to be the new owner's representative in North America. He was to be based in London for the first six or nine months and commute to Los Angeles on a weekly basis with a view to eventually moving to the company's offices on Wiltshire Boulevard. "That just sounded horrendous to me," says Hendry. "We were leaving Hong Kong on the basis that we wanted to put down some roots and have a normal life and I was going to spend most of my time flying across the Atlantic dealing with Americans who wouldn't take kindly to a Brit coming over and telling them how to run their company."

It was not until the end of 1987 that Hendry first heard about Coon. He was back in London talking to Eagle Star about his future when Ferguson told him about Coon's plans to start a life insurance company in New Zealand. Ferguson said Eagle Star was interested in the idea and that he wanted Hendry to go to New Zealand to assess the likelihood of the venture's success. Eagle Star had already sent one person on an earlier fact-finding visit but his report was confusing. The first nineteen and a half pages described why Coon's new life company would not succeed and then the last half page had recommended that Eagle Star go ahead with the investment anyway. Not surprisingly, Eagle Star's directors were not convinced and, in fact, wanted to drop the whole idea. But Ferguson was enthusiastic about Coon's project and did not want it to die so he suggested Hendry meet Coon and prepare a report that would convince the Board to approve the joint venture.

The trip was in fact Hendry's second visit to New Zealand. In early 1986, he had arrived with Ron Howroyd, then head of Eagle Star's international life business, to assess the opportunities for expansion into New Zealand because it was a market Eagle Star had not yet penetrated. Since Eagle Star had a very large Australian operation, New Zealand was a logical market for the company to enter. On that first trip, Hendry had met with a large number of insurance brokers and had come to the same conclusions as Coon had done; namely that the market was backward in terms of the insurance products that were available and the way in which the life business was conducted. He had found that advisors had reacted positively when told Eagle Star might introduce U.K. style life products into the New Zealand market. "They were incredibly enthusiastic," says Hendry. "They looked at the products and said, 'These are wonderful. We would dearly love to have access to them.'" Some of the advisors had been so excited by Hendry's visit that although Eagle Star decided not to open in New Zealand, they started selling Eagle Star's products anyway, placing their business through Hendry's Hong Kong office. Two of the first New Zealand brokers to do this were Laura and Okke Hansen and in 1989 when Sovereign opened its doors, they were among the very first brokers to recommend Sovereign's products to their clients.

Hendry arrived in New Zealand in the early part of 1988 and, like Coon, saw that the window of opportunity was still open.

Hendry arrived in New Zealand in the early part of 1988 and, like Coon, saw that the window of opportunity was still open. Not only did brokers continue to be excited about selling the new style products, but no new life companies had entered the New Zealand market for over twelve years and rationalisation was taking place within the industry. Capital Life had become part of NZI, Royal had merged with Sun Alliance, and Aetna had been taken over by Prudential. Most importantly, all the acquiring companies employed their own sales forces (called tied agents) and consequently there were fewer and fewer opportunities for independent brokers. The independent advisors were feeling squeezed out, insecure and poorly treated and Hendry believed they would enthusiastically support a new company that gave them the type of products and the level of service they craved.

It was on the 1988 trip that Hendry and Coon first met and they immediately hit it off. "Chris is an extremely positive person," says Hendry, "and a delightful person to work with. Even in that short time it was obvious we got on personally." Coon, for his part, needed little convincing that Hendry would make a good partner. "Duncan Ferguson had the highest regard for Ian," he recalls. "He said you couldn't get a better person to be involved in the marketing and administration side of the business. Duncan had 100% confidence in Ian and his word was good enough for me."

"I decided I should arrive on the eighth day of the eighth month of 1988, the most auspicious day that century according to the Chinese, because I was going to need all the luck I could get."

At the end of their first meeting, Coon and Hendry agreed that no matter what Eagle Star's verdict about becoming involved in Coon's venture might be, Hendry would consider coming back to New Zealand to be Coon's partner. Hendry actually made the decision to join Coon while at a worldwide insurance conference in Bangkok in May of 1988. "June and I discussed our future and neither of us wanted to go back to the U.K.," he says, "and neither of us wanted to get involved with the company in the States. So, we decided that whatever happened we were going to New Zealand, either with Eagle Star's blessing or without. This was a major decision for me because I had been with Eagle Star for 20 years and I had reached a position where my future prospects were very good. Throwing away 20 years of career development and long-term superannuation was a difficult decision but we decided that that was what we were going to do."

On his return to England, Hendry recommended Eagle Star invest in Coon's new life company but once again getting approval was difficult. Initially it had been Ferguson's intention that Eagle Star would take a 25 percent stake in the new venture with a view to taking control within five years. But Ferguson left Eagle Star in the middle of 1988 and his replacement took the view that since the money for the new venture would be coming out of Eagle Star's Australian operation, the final decision should be made by John Reid, the Australian general manager. Reid was in favour of the joint venture but corporate wheels grind slowly and he did not make the decision to invest in Coon's company until November of 1988 by which time Hendry had resigned from Eagle Star. As it turned out, when Eagle Star did finally come on board, it was in a lesser role. The company's rules required the Australian board to get approval from the parent company, British American Tobacco, if they were going to take more than a 10 percent stake holding in any company. "The Australian board," says Hendry grinning, "did not want to put itself in the position of trying to convince its parent company, which was preoccupied with its American problems, to throw a few hundred thousand dollars behind some lone Englishman wanting to start yet another life company in a place called New Zealand, so it opted to take only a 9.9% holding which it could do without anyone else's approval."

Slowly but surely, the power of Coon's vision and his determination to make it happen were turning his dream into reality. By early 1988, he had formed three key partnerships: one with two global re-insurance companies who could provide the necessary financing to support the company's growth, one with Eagle Star who would give his new company the credibility it needed, and one with Ian Hendry who had the marketing and operational skills Coon lacked and knew he would need if his company was to succeed. Originally, Hendry's role was to be marketing director. "I'd had enough of being a general manager," says Hendry. "I just wanted to concentrate on marketing which is my love." But he was to have this luxury for only a little over a year. It soon became clear to both of them that no one in the new organisation had the skills and experience to run the overall business and so Hendry, with some reluctance, took on the position of being director and general manager.

In mid 1988, Hendry was ready to move to New Zealand and get on with the job of launching Sovereign. "After spending six years in Hong Kong," he says, "I decided that if I was going to New Zealand to join a company that did not exist, had no office and no official name, I should arrive on the eighth day of the eighth month of 1988, the most auspicious day that century according to the Chinese, because I was going to need all the luck I could get." In reality, the

Hendry's arrived in the pouring rain and it continued to rain for the next three months. Also, within a week of arriving in New Zealand his briefcase containing all his Sovereign papers had been stolen. It was a taste of what was to come. Hendry was about to discover that building a life assurance company in New Zealand would be a never-ending struggle.

"Like all pioneers," says Hendry laughing, "we didn't have any idea of the magnitude of the task ahead."

CHAPTER 5

Piece by piece

"There was no marketing strategy of any kind. We had no staff. We had no computer systems. This was in August of 1988 and we were planning to open in less than five months."

If you asked Hendry and Coon how to build a successful business, they might reply, "The same way you eat an elephant - one piece at a time," since that is the way they built Sovereign. It was their intention to launch the new company on January 1st, 1989 and they realised there was a great deal to do if they were to meet that target. Although Coon had a detailed business plan and a clear idea of what the new products should look like, there was nothing on paper to describe them in any detail. "There was no marketing strategy of any kind," says Hendry shaking his head. "We had no staff and no computer systems. This was in August of 1988 and we were planning to open in less than five months." What they did have, however, was a strong relationship with Hurstmere Financial Services, an independent life agency operation run by John Scott and Mike Hodgkinson. Coon had become friendly with Scott in particular since arriving in New Zealand. Like others who listened to Coon's vision, he had become an enthusiastic supporter of Coon and his dream. After an unsatisfactory episode representing National Mutual (now AXA), Hurstmere was keen to align itself with the dynamic new company Coon had outlined.

Seeing Coon at work, huddled over his computer in his small attic bedroom office, Hendry decided that the first thing they needed was a proper business office. "One of the hardest things I had to do in the early days was actually get Chris out of his attic bedroom," he laughs. "He had an idyllic situation looking over the Gulf from his bedroom window and the idea of actually having to sit in a business office was not something Chris had any great enthusiasm for." Coon had been told that the new company would not be taken seriously unless it was located in Auckland's downtown area, but he decided that Sovereign would be based in Takapuna on Auckland's North Shore because he wanted to avoid the higher costs of being in the central business district. "I was concerned about costs," Coon says, "because everything was going on my credit card!"

One of the first places Coon and Hendry considered for the new company's home was the Post Office building on Hurstmere Road in Takapuna's central business district. It was here that Hendry lost his briefcase and all his papers including passports, credit cards, his daughter's school reports and the notes he had made in Hong Kong about the new start-up. The space they were looking at was on the top floor of the building at the end of a corridor. Hendry put his rather heavy case down at the beginning of the corridor and returned five minutes later to find it gone. "It was a complete shambles," he recalls with anguish. "I had just picked up the keys to my new house in Chatswood so one of the first things I had to do was get all the locks replaced. I was up all night phoning credit card companies in the U.K. asking them to cancel my cards and issue new ones. My daughter was trying to get into university and needed the certificates. It was a nightmare for the next couple of days." His daughter's papers were eventually found floating in the harbour off Devonport but other than someone trying to use one of his cards to buy liquor, nothing was ever seen of the case or its contents again. Not surprisingly, they were not impressed with the location. Instead, Sovereign's first office was to be 200 square feet on the second floor in what is today the J D Edwards Plaza. Coon and Hendry filled the office with furniture they brought from their homes and with some they picked up from a company that had gone bankrupt. Phone lines were installed and the company had a base and a physical address. All it needed now was a name!

"Sovereign was the name I thought fitted the bill because it suggested both strength and superior value."

Coon had toyed with a number of names, like Global Insurance, but Hendry thought they lacked impact. Looking back on those names, Coon agrees they were bland. "Yes, they were typical actuary's names," he admits with a laugh. Hendry had brainstormed all the names he could think of while he was still in Hong Kong, and had ended up with a list of more than 100 possibilities. He was looking for a name that sounded new and innovative but also traditional and stable. It had to have impact but sound respectable, and it had to be easy to remember, appropriate for New Zealand, and suggest quality. "*Sovereign* was the name I thought fitted the bill because it suggested both strength and superior value," says Hendry. "In fact the name I came up with was *Sovereign Alliance International Life* because I had this idea we wanted to form the acronym SAIL, being that Auckland is the City of Sails. Also, I liked the word *alliance* because it represented the alliance between Chris and me, and the alliance between Sovereign, Eagle Star and the reassurers." But when they tried to register this name with the Companies Office, Coon and Hendry were told they needed the permission of Sun Alliance because they had already registered the name, *Alliance* and the Companies Office was worried there could be a potential conflict. They expected no difficulty but to Hendry's disgust, Sun Alliance did object. "This was a bit ironic really because in the UK, where Sun Alliance is based, there were at least three insurance organisations which trade under the name of *Sun* or used the name *Alliance*, so for them to object to us using the name *Alliance* as being a secondary part of Sovereign I thought was a bit unreasonable," he says. Their second choice was *Sovereign Assurance* which both Coon and Hendry were concerned might seem a little too British or too Royalist to New Zealanders. But when they tested the name among advisers, it received a positive response. "Even now we get a strong positive response to the name," says Hendry. "It has everything we set out to incorporate in a name. It has a feeling of being solid and here for the long-term."

Ray Kroc, the founder of the McDonald's Corporation used to say: "Numbers are impressive, systems are effective, slogans are moving but people make it happen." Coon and Hendry shared that view and so with both a name and an office for the new company, they turned their attention to building a team. Hendry's daughter, Linda, became Sovereign's first staff member, helping out with clerical and administrative tasks while she waited for the next university year to start. The next person to join them was Maureen Hayter who became their secretary. Next on deck was Ernie Uganecz, a Canadian from Alberta. A large, jovial man with an outgoing personality, Uganecz's passion for the life industry in general, and for Sovereign in particular, is clear from the moment he starts talking. Uganecz looks and sounds like everyone's image of a very successful life assurance agent, which is exactly what he is. For 30 years, he worked for Sun Life of Canada, first in Canada, then in the Philippines and finally in the United States.

Uganecz grew up in the city of Edmonton. He enjoyed school but describes himself as having been an under-achiever in most subjects. After graduating with a degree in education from the University of Alberta, Uganecz taught junior high school but after one year he decided, as he tells it, "that the effort was not worth the compensation," and moved into an administrative job in the University of Alberta's Zoology Department. Originally, his intention was to do further studies at the same time but after a year he realised that as a part-time student it would take a long time to complete an advanced degree and he looked for something else to do.

One day, a neighbour who was a life agent, suggested that Uganecz might like to sell life insurance. "Sell life insurance? You've got to be kidding!" he replied, horrified at the thought. But the neighbour convinced him that his prejudices about the life industry might be wrong and that the job was at least worth looking into. Uganecz met with managers at two different companies and was impressed with what he saw. "They had a *real* building in the central business district with *real* people and telephones and desks," he recalls laughing.

"Sell life insurance? You've got to be kidding!"

His prejudices shattered, Uganecz went to work for Sun Life of Canada where he remained for the next three decades. During that time, Uganecz spent eight years in the field, at first selling, and later training new agents. He also worked at head office developing and delivering training programs. In fact, shortly after joining head office, he had a meeting with a senior vice-president and with characteristic bluntness told him Sun's training programs were "hopelessly out of date and irrelevant." Instead of getting fired, he got the job of improving them. Uganecz then spent the next three years developing a 22 module training program which is still used at Sun Life today.

Uganecz eventually became fed up with the bureaucracy and the internal politics of head office and since his wife, Jenny, is a Kiwi, they started thinking about moving to New Zealand. They had made several trips to New Zealand over the years and Uganecz liked both the country and the lifestyle it offered. As a step towards settling in New Zealand, in 1980 he successfully applied for a senior management position in the Philippines and then spent the next five years growing Sun Life's business in the Pacific region. "When I started we had 70 rag-tag agents," he recalls. "When I left, there were 450 hot agents in the business." But by 1985 things were getting uncomfortable for expatriates in Manila. "I had already been beaten up once at the airport," he recalls "and been told that I was an undesirable alien." Sun Life wanted their expatriate staff out and moved him to Boston. "If the years in Manila were the best in my life," Uganecz says, "then the years in Boston were the worst. It was an environment rife with bureaucracy and office politics - the very things I hate most and it was not helped by the attitude Americans have about Canadians coming in and telling them how to run their business!"

By 1986, Uganecz was becoming increasingly dissatisfied not only in Boston, but with Sun Life in general. He decided to work seriously towards his goal "to live in New Zealand on my terms with no reduction in lifestyle," he says chuckling. While he was in New Zealand on holidays that Christmas, he contacted several chief executives of major New Zealand life companies. One person he met with was Doug Leybourne, CEO of Metropolitan Life. "He asked me about my dreams," Uganecz recalls, "and I said I wanted to run my own insurance company. Then someone you should talk to, Leybourne told me, was Chris Coon." Two days later Uganecz and Coon had a 90-minute meeting that was to change Uganecz's life. "Chris told me about his dream and his vision for a new life company and the hairs on the back of my neck stood up," he says. "I recognised his vision, was excited by it and decided right then and there that I would be on his team if he would have me." For his part, Coon was taken with Uganecz's passion, energy and experience. He knew that if his company was to succeed he had to be able to convince independent agents to sell his products and to do that he was going to need someone with Uganecz's talents so although Uganecz returned to Boston, they kept in touch for the next eighteen months.

In October of 1988, Uganecz arrived in New Zealand to join Sovereign. On meeting him for the first time, Hendry could see the potential that Coon had seen. "He struck me as being a very outgoing, happy and pleasant person who had a great deal of relevant experience," he recalls. "Ernie is a great talker, a natural self-promoter. I believed that he would do a wonderful job of promoting Sovereign to the independent brokers in New Zealand." Like Coon and Hendry, Uganecz became one of Sovereign's founding shareholders although initially his role was unclear. "Chris had been the one involved in the discussions with Ernie and Chris can be very vague at times," says Hendry with a smile. "I knew Ernie was coming but I didn't know in what capacity." After he arrived, the three of them quickly decided that since Uganecz's skills were in managing an agency force, he should set up Caledonian Financial Services, which was to be Sovereign's wholly owned network of advisors. Although Coon and

Hendry believed independent advisors would be keen to sell Sovereign's revolutionary products, they decided to hedge their bets by developing their own advisor network as well. This was not to be a group of tied agents who could sell only Sovereign products since all three believed that tied agencies were a thing of the past. Rather it was to be a group of independent brokers who would sell Sovereign products only if they found them to be the best value for both their clients and themselves. This was a radical departure from the norm in the industry at that time since all the major players in the market, such as National Mutual, AMP, Metropolitan Life, Sun Alliance, Prudential, Norwich, Government Life, and Colonial were using their own tied agency force as the primary means of distributing their products.

Uganecz remained with Sovereign for nearly 11 years until he 'retired' in 1999. Today, a large number of brokers in the New Zealand life industry owe much of their success to the skills, knowledge and coaching Uganecz gave them. From the company's point of view, Uganecz has been the voice of Sovereign. No one has done more to tell the world about Coon's dream. Always passionate about the ideals and philosophies Sovereign represented, he has been the company's biggest champion, helping New Zealanders to understand Sovereign's radical approach to life assurance.

By the end of 1988, with an office, a company name, and the beginnings of a team in place, and brimming with confidence, Coon and Hendry set out to change New Zealand's life assurance industry. "I believed very firmly that Sovereign would be successful and I guess I didn't appreciate some of the risks quite as clearly as other people," Coon admits. Hendry agrees. "In the early months, we couldn't see any obstacles in our path," he says. Their optimism was not, however, shared by everyone they approached, especially those whose products or services they wished to buy. Since the stock market crash of '87 was still fresh in people's minds, every potential supplier they met, from marketing consultants through to lawyers and accountants, had the same thought in their minds as they listened to these two enthusiastic newcomers passionately describe their plans to begin a new life assurance company. "Will these people be able to pay us?" was the question on everyone's lips. Several companies actually declined the Sovereign business, a decision they must surely regret since many of those who did take the risk were still doing business with Sovereign 10 years later. For some that has amounted to hundreds of thousands of dollars worth of business. Nearly all those who did agree to become

Sovereign's suppliers in the early days followed the same initial strategy. They did a little work, got the bill in quickly and waited to see whether they got paid. They always did.

The first supplier Coon and Hendry sought was a marketing consultant. Several firms were approached before Coon and Hendry found one they believed they could work with. Some of those approached declined to take the risk of dealing with a new company, while others suggested campaigns that went against the grain. One company, for example, proposed an advertising campaign based on the slogan 'good as gold,' a New Zealand cliché that was being used by many other companies at the time. "They came up with the concept of cartoon characters such as Old King Cole, throwing gold sovereigns all over the place," says Hendry. "It was dreadful. It certainly wasn't an image that reflected the type of company we wanted to develop."

Through a mutual friend, Hendry and Coon were introduced to Kaye Coyne and Dwight Whitney, consultants in marketing, advertising and communications. Coyne had worked for Marac Finance and therefore had a very good understanding of how to launch a new financial service company. They met in October of 1988 at Sovereign's office. When they arrived for the meeting, Hendry and Uganecz were not there and Coon was so engrossed in working on his computer that he did not notice they had arrived. Eventually the meeting started and, in spite of a poor first impression, Coyne and Whitney were struck by both the dream and the dreamers. And dreamers they seemed to be. "It was October. They told us they wanted to launch in January, but they had no products and no identity. All they had were a few ideas," says Whitney. "But we could see that they were very serious and they wanted to get going right away." Coyne and Whitney accepted the challenge of getting ready for the launch, and after being pleased with their preliminary work, Coon and Hendry appointed them as Sovereign's marketing consultants. For 11 years, Coyne and Whitney were responsible for the development and protection of the Sovereign image. Indeed, the success of the Sovereign brand is largely due to Coyne and Whitney's expertise (see Chapter 14), which is what Coon and Hendry expected. But little did they know when they appointed

"It was October. They told us they wanted to launch in January, but they had no products and no identity. All they had were a few ideas."

them as marketing consultants that Sovereign's survival would be dependent on Coyne's understanding of how New Zealand's regulators operate, and on the contacts she had among the legal fraternity.

> *"They came back to me and said, 'How would you like to be an underwriter with a brand new insurance company?' and I thought it all sounded too disgusting."*

With the marketing work under way, the next step was to find a commercial law firm and a chartered accountant to ensure Sovereign complied with all statutory requirements. Ernst & Young became Sovereign's accountants and Hesketh Henry became Sovereign's legal advisers. Long time employees of Sovereign often joke that Eric Bachmann, the new man in Hesketh Henry who was appointed to look after the Sovereign account, has made a career from keeping Hendry out of jail. Bachmann has indeed been instrumental in Sovereign's success. "He has been extremely supportive and has really guided us through the minefield we've been walking in for the past 12 years," says Hendry.

Coon and Hendry acknowledge that they have not made life easy for any of their suppliers. "We have been a difficult problem for all the people that we've dealt with because in all respects we are quite different from other companies. The way we are structured, the way we're financed, the way that we think, the types of products we sell, our approach to sales and distribution, it's all so very different from what these companies were used to. Nobody here had come across a company like us before and they have had to learn as they went along. It has really been a difficult learning process for many of them," Coon explains.

After sourcing their key suppliers, Uganecz focused on establishing Caledonian Financial Services and Coon and Hendry turned their attention once again to putting people and systems in place to process applications, policies, and claims. With Maureen and Linda running the office, Coon and Hendry's first priority was to find an underwriter who could process policy applications and issue policies. They approached an employment agency that introduced them to a young dark-haired woman who, like themselves, was an idealist. For the past seven years, Naomi Ballantyne had been working in Auckland at Fidelity Insurance but she had become increasingly disillusioned with the insurance industry. "I had made a decision to get out of life insurance in New Zealand," she recalls, "primarily because the industry was focused on what was best for the company not on what was best for the customer. As a result, in my role as underwriter I was constantly explaining to people decisions that I didn't believe in. I found it extremely difficult to accept that." As a way out, Ballantyne listed herself with an employment agency, hoping to gain entry into another industry. It did not work out that way. "They came back to me and said, 'How would you like to be an underwriter with a brand new insurance company?' and I thought it all sounded too disgusting," says Ballantyne with a laugh. Nevertheless, she went along for an interview with Coon and Hendry and found them, as everyone else had done, crammed into their little office in the North City Plaza along with Linda, two desks, a guest chair and their dream.

It did not take Ballantyne long to change her mind about leaving the life assurance industry. "Just listening to Chris and Ian talk about what they saw as the future for the company they were planning to start really excited me," she says, her eyes shining brightly. "It was exciting for two reasons. Sovereign was a new company, not an existing traditional life insurance company so the opportunities that I would have in developing my own career were pretty exciting. But most important was how much control I would have over what I was doing, especially in how we would handle our clients. That's what excited me the most."

If Ballantyne was impressed with Coon and Hendry, the feeling was mutual. What they saw was a young enthusiastic capable woman with a bubbly personality, a sharp mind and a good sense of humour who became as excited about the Sovereign dream as they were. Seeing past her youthfulness (she was only 24 at the time), they quickly recognised her experience and skills, and they were particularly impressed with her forthright style. They discovered, too, that her ideas about running a life business and developing a customer-driven company culture were the same as their own. "We both knew we had found the right person," says Coon. "We didn't even need to leave the room to talk about it. We just looked at each other and I offered her the job there and then." She became Sovereign's first manager and stayed with the company for nearly 12 years.

Finding Ballantyne was a piece of luck, but recognising the talent, igniting the enthusiasm with their vision and, over the years, giving her the autonomy and support to use her abilities was inspired leadership. During her time with Sovereign, Ballantyne, as even her detractors will admit, played an instrumental role in the company's success. "She was worth her weight in gold," says Coon. "She was very well organised and very direct. If there was a problem she would roll her sleeves up and get stuck in. Naomi was incredibly reliable, very efficient but also very humane." Ballantyne was as passionate and excited about the Sovereign dream when she left the company in 2001 as she was when she joined. Regarded by everyone as 'the keeper of the culture', during her time at Sovereign she strove to keep the original vision in the forefront of everyone's mind. She worked tirelessly to create an organisation that was customer driven, efficient, innovative, team-based and a fun place to work. Most importantly, she worked to make Sovereign a place where people took responsibility for their work and had pride in their performance. "My goal was to build a team of confident, skilled and motivated people who operated world class systems," says Ballantyne, "and I believe we achieved that."

Ballantyne is a woman of very high standards and high energy, and never satisfied with the status quo, she worked constantly to improve service levels and to drive innovation and change. She was always on the look out for new ideas, and as a result was the main instigator of many of the innovations that have made Sovereign the company that other New Zealand life companies envy. Although for many years Ballantyne carried the title of operations director, she was also Sovereign's chief trouble-shooter. When the staff of MetLife had to be integrated into Sovereign, Ballantyne was given the job. When there were problems with New Zealand Superannuation Services, she was sent in to sort out the mess.

When Ballantyne joined Sovereign in November of 1988, she found there was a lot to do. "We had nothing," she recalls. "We had no policies, no systems, no paperwork, no computer systems. We had absolutely nothing." Her first direction from Coon was to design a proposal form, medical report forms and to develop a process for handling new business. Since Coon and Hendry planned to start selling life insurance policies in January of 1989, Ballantyne had less than eight weeks to get things up and running. "When she first joined us, we were starting to panic as we were under considerable pressure from Hurstmere, a large Auckland-based firm of independent advisers, which had a team of brokers and no product to sell," Coon admits. "We could see what had to be done and thought it would take three or four months to complete everything. Naomi finished it all in two weeks and came back asking for more to do."

The lease at North City Plaza was for only three months and during that time, it became obvious that larger premises were needed. In November of 1988, Sovereign took 1800 square feet on the top floor of 17 Anzac Street in Takapuna. In three months, the fledgling company had increased its space sevenfold and nearly quadrupled its staff. Coon's dream was definitely becoming reality.

> *Ballantyne had less than eight weeks to get things up and running.*

Coon and Hendry recognised that if Ballantyne was to run an efficient operations section then Sovereign needed a computer system. "We appreciated that the computer system was critical. We had to have a basic system in place as soon as possible that could actually pay some commission, print a policy and collect the next month's direct debits," says Coon. Thus, they went in search of a data processing manager and found Don Jefferies. Jefferies had worked in computers with insurance companies and had also done a stint with a computer software company that specialised in developing systems for life companies. He was just the man Coon and Hendry were looking for. Jefferies was skilled in computers and software, and knowledgeable about the life industry. But he was doubtful about joining Sovereign. "I really didn't give the company much chance of succeeding," he recalls, "but since I was without a job, I figured I didn't have much to lose. Besides, part of me was attracted to the chance of being part of a start-up company in the life industry." Like the others, he could see so much opportunity to do things better than traditional companies were doing. Jefferies joined Sovereign in December of 1988 and quickly set about working with Ballantyne to build computer systems to process policy applications. By now there were fewer than three working weeks before Sovereign's doors were scheduled to open for business. Jefferies met the deadline by designing a system based on one he had worked with previously, one that was good enough to get them through the first six months. By then Sovereign had grown so quickly that it had to be replaced with a more sophisticated system.

Like Ballantyne, Jefferies embraced the Sovereign philosophy of providing superior customer service. His approach to developing data processing systems was to work in partnership with operations to develop systems that did what they needed to have done in the way they wanted done. "This was different from the way most life companies operated," explains Jefferies with pride. "Usually data processing systems are developed to serve company policy not the people working in the company, and certainly not the company's customers. Compared to existing companies we were outstanding." This was not an empty boast. Jefferies and Ballantyne instituted performance measures of such critical indicators as speed, productivity and cycle time. Their results showed clearly that Sovereign became an industry leader very early on.

Coon and Hendry had a lot to show for just over four months of work.

With an office, a name, four full-time staff, relationships with key suppliers, forms, processes, and data processing systems, and the beginnings of an independent insurance brokerage, Coon and Hendry had a lot to show for just over four months work.

But most importantly, during this time, they had developed the hottest insurance products ever to hit the New Zealand market.

CHAPTER 6

Hot products, hot service

"We started with a quiet determination and belief that our introduction of a special blend of products and services, elements of which had been tried and tested in other parts of the world, would be well received by New Zealanders. It was our aim to create an organisation that did not have a wieldy infrastructure and was capable of responding to changing market conditions and needs."

The strategy was simple: build the right products, be different and provide significantly better service than the competition. Coon and Hendry not only built the right products, they shook up the life industry in New Zealand, simply by introducing refinements of products that were commonplace overseas but which New Zealand life companies had chosen not to make available to New Zealand consumers.

Twelve years ago, Coon and Hendry understood what many business leaders today have still not grasped: a competitive advantage is not gained by trying to run the fastest in the same race as everyone else, but rather by inventing your own race. Coon and Hendry believed Sovereign needed to provide its customers with brand new products that were very different from what was currently available in New Zealand. "The products we designed incorporated a range and blend of desirable elements we found were deficient in the traditional 'with bonus' and so-called 'capital guaranteed' products that the majority of companies in New Zealand were marketing," says Coon, "and that meant giving customers access to a wide range of internationally based investment products. It also meant developing products that were attractively priced and had built-in flexibility so they never became obsolete."

The first priority was given to developing financial service products. "Our whole thought to start with was to be investment oriented and international in outlook because we recognised a major shortcoming of the local market was investing only in New Zealand. If people did invest abroad, it was in Australia which really was another primary producer country," Coon explains. Rather than hire their own team of fund managers, as most insurance companies and financial services organisations were doing, Sovereign's strategy was to give Sovereign's customers direct access to a wide range of international funds that were diversified both as to the type of fund and the geographic area of the investment. Coon and Hendry knew Sovereign could never afford the cost of hiring and equipping a team of investment advisers and, even more importantly, they knew that no matter how large the team was its expertise would be limited. Both these problems could be overcome, they realised, if investors could use the expertise of some of the world's top fund managers who were, in effect, competing with each other. Not only would this give investors access to a wide range of talent but the competitive environment would keep the fund managers on their toes and ensure that investors' savings were placed only in top-performing funds. The network Coon and Hendry put in place included international institutions such as Perpetual, Fidelity, Rothschilds, GT, Hambros, Guiness Flight, Flemings and Bankers Trust, in addition to using local funds such as Mace, BNZ and Nathans. "We were trying to achieve two things by setting up this independent fund management network," explains Coon. "One was to get performance, because the companies we identified had demonstrated an ability to perform over long periods in different market conditions, but the secondary objective was to add another layer of credibility onto what we were doing by virtue of our association with these very significant international institutions." To oversee the investment side of Sovereign's business, Coon and Hendry formed an Investment Strategy and Management Group which included Sovereign management and Arun Abey of Nathan Funds Management Limited, a joint venture between Lion Nathan and IPAC Securities Group, one of Australasia's most widely respected research houses. This group's role was to select the funds that would be used, develop structures for using them and monitor each fund's performance. This team was highly effective in selecting and structuring investment options for Sovereign's customers and the performance of the funds selected was extremely good. UK unit trusts were the preferred investment vehicle because of the tax advantages they provide by not requiring tax on gains to be paid until

> *The strategy was simple: build the right products, be different and provide significantly better service than the competition.*

the investment is realised. "By investing in equities using UK unit trusts, it meant the fund manager could buy and sell all the underlying investments and we didn't actually pay any tax on the gains until we finally sold the units. Since when one policyholder matures we replace him with another policyholder, it meant our selling of the units could be a very long way away in the future. Effectively, one got a gross roll-up," says Coon.

In its first year of operation, Sovereign launched three products under the *Sovereign Lifestyle Product Portfolio.* Coon had been working on these for several years, taking products widely used in the UK, refining them based on his experience, and adapting them to New Zealand conditions. Then when Hendry joined him, the two worked in earnest to package them for launching in January 1989. Marketed as separate products, they were really just variations of one product in Coon's mind. "I had always seen them as being just one plan," says Coon, "that reflected our strategy of giving the New Zealand consumer access to global investments, under flexible arrangements and at a competitive price." In keeping with Sovereign's strategy for investment products, each of these became a door through which ordinary New Zealanders could access the world's top investment funds and fund managers, which had up until then been available only to investors with large sums of money. Moreover, these products gave investors the opportunity to diversify their portfolio over a wide range of fund types and through different parts of the world.

The three products, *Homeplan 1000, Investor Plus* and the *Sovereign Investment Bond,* were spectacular performers. The strategy of using competing international fund managers proved to be particularly successful. Sovereign's investment funds were top performers, winning best performing fund awards for four of its funds and also top performing fund overall out of 74 funds monitored by an independent researcher. "Our fund performance left the rest of the industry in the starting blocks," says Coon with pride. "The results of our managed Conservative, Balanced Growth and Performance funds have shown the benefits of our independent, professional, and diversified approach to fund management."

Homeplan 1000 was a mortgage-based product that provided a fresh approach to financing property purchases by using a life assurance plan. Basically, this was a UK concept for providing home loans, which was unknown in New Zealand. The type of mortgage traditionally used by New Zealanders is the table mortgage. This mortgage is linked to a particular property and has level payments spread over the term of the mortgage. The main disadvantage of a table mortgage is that in the early years these payments are used primarily to pay off interest with most of the principal not being repaid until the latter part of the term. Also, with a table mortgage, when the property is sold the mortgage must be paid off and another mortgage taken out on the new property. Thus if people move several times over their lifetimes, they are doing little more than paying interest. *Homeplan 1000,* on the other hand, consisted of two parts: an interest only loan, which in Sovereign's case was initially provided by the National Australia Bank (NAB), and a *Homeplan* life policy, designed to accumulate cash that could be used to repay the mortgage at the end of the term. Indeed, based on the rate of return for investments current at that time, policyholders could expect to have a significant cash surplus after repaying the interest-only loan at the expiration of the policy. Another benefit of *Homeplan 1000* was that the mortgage was portable, meaning it could be transferred from house to house. Thus the mortgagor could buy and sell property as much as they liked and still allow the mortgage to run to the end of its term.

> *"I always found it extremely hard to understand why someone should actually pay a fee for the privilege of buying a bank product because in the UK, the market was so competitive that no one was charging fees."*

Homeplan 1000 was also unusual in that it had no fees. "I always found it extremely hard to understand why someone should actually pay a fee for the privilege of buying a bank product because at that time, in the UK, the market was so competitive that no one was charging fees," says Hendry. "I felt this was one area where we could gain a competitive advantage if we could get a bank to agree to allow us access to their mortgage funds without the borrower having to pay a fee." Coon and Hendry approached the NAB with their concept because Coon had met the NAB people in London and they had given him the name of Peter Taylor in New Zealand. Taylor was originally from the UK and therefore had an understanding of the type of mortgages Coon and Hendry had in mind. Initially the bank was cool to the no fee idea but Coon and Hendry found an ally in Toby Potter, a business development executive at NAB. Eventually the bank agreed to waive all fees and also offer a concessionary interest rate one-quarter of a per cent below standard market rates.

With the expected growth in *Homeplan* business, Coon and Hendry were anxious to employ a mortgage manager and approached Ross Wallace. Wallace was not easy to recruit. He was working for Securities Corporation in the office next door to Sovereign on Anzac Street and, since he had a steady job, he had reservations about joining a start-up company which may or may not have mortgages for him to process. Once again, Coon and Hendry were able to sell Sovereign on the strength of their dream and Wallace came on board. Since the bank saw Wallace as being a professional mortgage man, they were happy for Sovereign to take responsibility for the quality control of the mortgage applications that would be sent to the bank. As it turned out, Sovereign's screening process was so effective that only a small percentage of mortgage applications were ever rejected by the bank. For their part, Coon and Hendry were delighted to work with the National Australia Bank. "The combination of their interest rate, no fee and our wonderful product was a very attractive package," says Hendry. "We made very rapid strides in developing the product and introducing it into the market place."

Investor Plus was an investment product designed to provide New Zealanders with the opportunity to build a substantial cash fund through a flexible savings plan. This plan would give Sovereign's policyholders access to a wide-range of international managed and specialist funds operated by some of the world's leading financial institutions. *Investor Plus* gave even small investors who had only $50 per month or $600 per year to contribute, access to global funds that were previously the domain of only those with large sums of money to invest. It was a product with a high degree of flexibility. Premium payments could be made on a regular basis or in a lump sum, clients could determine the risk profile of their investments, and they could increase or decrease their contributions as their personal circumstances changed. They could even suspend contributions for up to 12 months without loss of benefits. At the end of the term, policyholders would receive a lump sum. The insurance component of *Investor Plus* provided death cover, accidental death cover and travel accidental death cover, in addition to a waiver of premium and a regular income benefit in the case of disability. The policy also contained a built-in inflation proofing facility. Like *Homeplan* 1000, this product was an instant hit with advisors and policyholders alike for both its versatility and its performance.

The third major product Coon and Hendry introduced was the *Sovereign Investment Bond,* a highly flexible lump sum savings plan which also gave policyholders access to the world's top investment funds. For a minimum of $2,000, contributors could choose to invest in any four of the 12 funds offered by Sovereign. The *Sovereign Investment Bond* was also very flexible. Investors could change their entire portfolio at any time to take advantage of changing local or global economic conditions. It also had a life insurance component equal to 101% of the value of the investment at the time of death.

Coon and Hendry were confident their UK style products would take the market place by storm. "We started with a quiet determination and a belief that our special blend of products and services, which had elements that had been tried and tested in other parts of the world, would be well received by New Zealanders," says Coon. But Coon and Hendry also knew that superior products alone would not be enough to succeed in the coming decade. Sovereign would have to deliver superior service to both advisors and policyholders if they were to realise their dream. This was where their opportunity to gain a competitive advantage would lie because the uncertainty created by rationalisation within the life industry was alienating many agents from the companies that remained, and because those companies were treating their sales forces abysmally. Coon and Hendry knew that these experienced salespeople were feeling resentful and anxious, and they felt sure they would respond positively to a new innovative company that was prepared to do things differently. Thus they set out to create an organisation that was dynamic and innovative, one that could respond quickly to market conditions and needs because it did not have an unwieldy infrastructure and a legacy of tradition hanging around its neck like the established companies did.

"Service is the culture on which Sovereign is built," says Hendry and he has never wavered from that view. Right from the beginning, everyone at Sovereign knew there was only one acceptable way to deal with advisors and policyholders and that was to be fast, fair and efficient. "Once we started selling policies, the way we dealt with brokers and eventually with clients was consistently ethical," Ballantyne recalls, "and that's the one thing about Sovereign that really inspires the loyalty of its staff. We could all live with, and believe in, the way we were expected to deal with other people. It was just such a breath of fresh air compared to the insurance industry in New Zealand which in my experience was concerned with how they can get as much money as possible from their clients without having to give too much in return." The main Sovereign value, which comes directly from the strongly held values of Coon and Hendry, was, "If it is the right thing to do, then do it. We'll worry about the profitability later." That philosophy extended to everyone within Sovereign and also to the advisors who represented the company.

By the end of 1988, revolutionary products were ready for the marketplace, key staff had been appointed, marketing material had been prepared and rudimentary systems had been developed. And, rudimentary they were indeed. There were, for example, no policy maintenance systems in place. All the administrative systems could do was issue a policy. Initially staff had to calculate rates manually from a rates book although shortly after that the information was available to them on disk.

There was only one small obstacle between Coon and Hendry and success. They had few customers and, apart from Hurstmere, no distribution channels. "Our main objective was to get brokers," says Hendry. "We knew that without a national network of brokers, we didn't have a viable business."

CHAPTER 7

Have Yellow Pages will travel

"They were exciting times. We were a small group of people battling the odds. It was a good time - a fun time."

The primary customers of an insurance company without a salaried sales force are the independent advisers and brokers who sell its products to the public. Coon and Hendry knew all along that building relationships with these people was absolutely critical to Sovereign's success. They had decided right from the beginning that a tied agency force, where agents were on salary, housed in company offices and supported by the company's secretaries and managers, was not the best strategy. Nearly all the established life insurance companies in New Zealand were selling their policies that way, but Coon, Hendry and Uganecz could all see that the days of tied agency forces were numbered. 'Green peas', as advisors new to the business are called, are expensive to recruit and train, and an agency force is costly to house and manage. Moreover, the turnover rate is very high, particularly in the first years. Having a tied agency force is therefore a very expensive way of distributing a life company's products and, in a competitive market full of price-sensitive customers, it is an increasingly unprofitable way of doing business. For Sovereign, in particular, a tied agency force made no sense. As a start-up company, Sovereign could ill-afford the huge cost of putting a salaried sales force in place. "I'd had the experience of trying to develop a life sales force in Hong Kong," Hendry recalls, "and I knew how difficult that was. I also knew how expensive it was and I knew it was a long-term project because the attrition rate is horrendous. I had seen the targets in Chris's business plan and I realised it was going to take years for us to get to the point where we would have a strong enough agency force to get anywhere close to meeting them."

Moreover, there was no need. During the 1980s, a number of insurance companies merged leaving a large number of advisers without a home. Even more importantly, most established companies in New Zealand were treating their agents and the independent brokers with little respect. They certainly did not see their agents as their customers but merely as employees who could be told what to do. As a result, there were many dissatisfied agents eager to deal with a company who would treat them differently. "From my trip to New Zealand in 1986," Hendry says, "I knew there were some very good and very professional brokers who could give us instant access to the market. It made sense to use these brokers as our national network and let them promote the company."

Hendry, Coon and Uganecz decided that their sales strategy would be two-pronged. Firstly, they would attempt to persuade existing independent advisors to sell Sovereign's products. They thought this would be relatively easy because of the way the independents were being treated by the established life companies, and because of the attractiveness of Sovereign's products. They also understood, however, that advisers would need to be convinced that Sovereign was financially stable before they would recommend its products. They would be very cautious about risking their client's money with a new, as yet unproven, company. This is where Coon and Hendry planned to use their connections with both Eagle Star and their reassurers. The second prong to their strategy was to start their own independent force. This was to be Uganecz's task. He would use his 30 years experience to build an independent, but wholly owned company, called Caledonian Financial Services. Caledonian agents would be commission only sales people, and would be free to sell the products of any life company in New Zealand. But Coon, Hendry and Uganecz believed that Sovereign would get the lion's share of Caledonian's business because of the superiority of its products and because of the quality of the service Sovereign would give both advisors and policyholders alike.

Developing the first strategy of persuading existing advisers to sell Sovereign's products was to be Hendry's responsibility. The challenging task of building relationships with independent brokers throughout New Zealand was made easier with the recruitment of David Whyte, an exuberant outgoing man who, never one to mince his words, would quickly become as passionate an advocate for Sovereign as Coon, Hendry, Uganecz and Ballantyne. By coincidence, at one time Whyte, like Hendry, had also worked for Eagle Star, and in Glasgow no less. But although Whyte had heard about Hendry, the two had never met. Like most of the other expatriates at Sovereign, Whyte also had a Kiwi connection through his wife who had relatives living in New Zealand. They had made several trips to New Zealand and were attracted by the same lifestyle features that had attracted both Coon and Uganecz. After being in New Zealand for the Rugby World Cup in 1987, Whyte decided to make New Zealand home. He went back to Aberdeen, sold the brokerage he had been running for ten years, and emigrated.

Once in New Zealand, Whyte saw the same opportunity for a new life company that would do things differently as Coon had done, so he wrote to Eagle Star recommending they start an operation in New Zealand. The letter was sent to John Douglas, someone Hendry knew very well. Douglas replied promptly, advising Whyte to talk to Hendry. "David found it hard to believe," says Hendry, "that someone he had heard so much about in Glasgow in 1974 was sitting in Auckland in 1988 doing what he was recommending be done. We met and it didn't take very long for us to realise that he had the skills we needed, and that we could provide the challenge he was looking for." At the time of their meeting, Whyte was working in the financial services division at Countrywide Bank. He remembers that he and Hendry had a very guarded conversation on the phone to set up their meeting. Each could see the business opportunity that existed in the New Zealand life industry but neither knew how much the other was aware of the potential. They met, realised they had a common vision, and believed they could work well together. Whyte left Countrywide and joined Sovereign as broker development manager on December 20, 1988. Two days later, Coon and Hendry posted the half million-dollar bond required by the Justice Department to establish a life company.

Thanks to the relationship Coon had developed with Hurstmere, Hendry and Whyte did not have to start building a broker network from scratch. In 1987, Hurstmere were selling policies underwritten by Capital Life, but when New Zealand Insurance acquired Capital Life, their best selling product disappeared leaving the owners of Hurstmere with a successful company but no products. At that time, National Mutual was using its chequebook to expand its agency network and so, in return for a large sum of money and on the understanding that National Mutual would develop a product similar to the one that NZI had killed, Hurstmere agreed to become tied agents of National Mutual. But National Mutual never did produce the promised product and for twelve months Hurstmere had nothing to sell. During this period, Coon met John Scott, Mike Hodgkinson and Alex Fowler, the principals of Hurstmere, and discussed his ideas for new life insurance products. Like everyone Coon talked to, they were both excited about his plans and agreed to sell his products as soon as they were available.

Sovereign opened for business in January 1989, with their new products and marketing material in place, with at least rudimentary policy documents and systems developed, and with the beginnings of a national distribution network through Hurstmere and the infant Caledonian Financial Services. Hendry and Coon expected a flurry of activity but they did not understand the New Zealand culture. "We all turned up for work on the first working day of January, 1989 and couldn't understand why the phones weren't ringing and why nobody was rushing to our door to buy a policy," says Hendry. "It was probably another week before we realised that New Zealand was still at the beach." In the event, it was the end of January of 1989 before anything started to happen. The 'great Kiwi shut down,' as Hendry calls it, frustrated Sovereign's first month in business and it drives him to distraction to this day. To everyone's amusement, he is forever trying to find ways to encourage advisors to start work early in January, always without success.

The first broker to present a proposal for a policy was Glen Halford, an adviser with many years of industry experience. Halford was introduced to Sovereign by Ballantyne, who had worked with him when she was at Fidelity. "I remember the first proposal we received," says Ballantyne. "It was delivered by the broker himself and accepted by me personally. I underwrote it manually, typed the policy and sent it out the door the same day." In the first year, 25% to 30% of Sovereign's business came from Hurstmere. But Hendry knew he could not rely on one source for such a large proportion of his sales and, as it turned out, he was right. "The problem," says Hendry, "was that the principals at Hurstmere had the expectation they would be the sole distribution channel for Sovereign's products. From our point of view, this was quite unrealistic." This difference in expectation caused increasing conflict between Hurstmere and Sovereign. Their relationship gradually deteriorated and was finally terminated in the mid 1990s.

> *Their strategy was simple. Hendry and Whyte would choose a town on the map, go there, get out the Yellow Pages, find the brokers and go to see them.*

To build a broader advisor base, Hendry and Whyte set out to talk to every broker they could find. They had no doubts about how they would be received. "We were sufficiently arrogant to believe that we had something that people would immediately recognise as being better than anything else that was available. And, we really believed that from day one people would look at us and say, 'These guys know what they are doing, have got great products, I can relate to this,'" says Hendry. The two started in Auckland with advisors closest to home, then packed their bags and travelled New Zealand, eventually covering the whole country knocking on brokers' doors. "For some time, David and I hunted as a team," Hendry recalls, "and, of course, we very quickly got the reputation as being the Scottish Mafia." David's picture of those times is more swashbuckling. " It was like the musketeers out there," he says. "You were fencing with guys who were basically armed with old cutlasses while you had a rapier which was faster, sharper, easier to handle and certainly more flexible than anything the opposition had."

Their strategy was simple. Hendry and Whyte would choose a town on the map, go there, get out the Yellow Pages, find the brokers and go to see them. "I must say, we were very well organised," says Hendry. "We had a clear strategy as to how we would tackle the country and we had put together a substantial list of brokers. With Linda's help, we went through the phone directories, both the White Pages and the Yellow Pages, because there was no comprehensive database or central listing. The brokers had no association which they all belonged to. They were just a lot of individuals in business independently. We wasted a lot of effort trying to find people who had died, sold their businesses, gone bankrupt in the Crash or moved elsewhere." The whole exercise was made harder, of course because all four of them, Coon, Hendry, Uganecz and Whyte, were newcomers to New Zealand. They were, however, able to get a list of brokers associated with Capital Life from John Thompson a former Capital employee who had left to run his own insurance brokerage, and so Capital's former brokers became the first group Hendry and Whyte targeted.

But finding brokers was only half the battle. It was not always easy to persuade them to start writing Sovereign business. "One of the great frustrations we had in the first four years," says Hendry, "is that we would be able to talk to brokers, and excite them about our concepts and our products, but we could not get them to write business because they were financially dependent on another company. These people positioned themselves as independent brokers when in fact they were not independent in any sense of the word." Another problem they had was that having found a willing broker,

Hendry and Whyte also had to make an assessment about whether this was a broker they could trust and who worked to the same principles and standards as they did. Coon had learned in England the dangers of dealing with shoddy advisors who wrote poor quality business that would never stay on the books. But knowing the dangers and knowing the advisors were two different things, however. "We knew about some people's reputations but we were really babes in the woods," Hendry admits. "We had nobody we could really approach to get information about any individual broker. We had to make our own assessment of people as we met them, and that is extremely difficult to do. You can't really tell whether someone is honest, trustworthy and reliable on the basis of a couple of conversations, so we entered into many relationships in good faith hoping for the best. Inevitably we developed some relationships, which, with the benefit of hindsight, we wished we hadn't. Then we had to work to extricate ourselves from them."

In the early days, Sovereign found itself doing business with some brokers who were either rogues or incompetents, including some of their biggest producers. Brokers of dubious character saw the fledgling company run by the newly arrived foreigners as being a rip-off waiting to happen. "We were like lambs to the slaughter," Hendry says with a grimace. But not all the advisors acted with premeditated malice. Many, including some of the larger brokerages, were just run by poor business operators who, like many small business owners, had serious cash flow problems. Such brokers cost Sovereign over $3 million in their first four years of operation!

Sovereign was selling 5% of all the new policies sold in New Zealand within six months of opening, a target they thought would take five years to reach.

In spite of the problems finding advisers, having to make cold calls and the risks of making a bad decision, Hendry and Whyte were having fun. "They were exciting times," says Hendry. "We were a small group of people battling the odds. It was a good time, a fun time." They were doing something each had spent almost their entire working life mastering, and they had absolute confidence in their products. They had been convinced beyond a shadow of doubt that Sovereign's revolutionary products would be received enthusiastically by both advisors and consumers, and they were right. Coon's business plan called for Sovereign to be selling 5% of all the new policies sold in New Zealand by its fifth year of operation, and they achieved this target in their first six months of being in business! "Sovereign sand-bagged the existing life companies because they had the best products and the best service. We looked after the brokers like no one ever had, and all the opposition could do was retaliate by trying to handcuff the independent advisers," drawls Whyte in his strong Scottish accent, his eyes flashing with glee.

Hendry and Coon had rushed to launch Sovereign because they believed that opportunities existed due to the changes that were taking place within the life industry in New Zealand. Whyte saw it that way, too. "The climate was right, the timing was right and the external environment was right for what we were doing," says Whyte. "And with brilliant foresight and strategic planning on our part," he adds with a laugh, "the day Sovereign opened, Aetna Life disappeared." Aetna's takeover by Prudential created a huge opportunity for Sovereign. Aetna, having no sales force of its own, had relied solely on independent advisers to sell its products. Prudential, on the other hand, had a tied agency force and when Prudential acquired Aetna it was not interested in looking after the independents. "When Prudential took over," says Whyte, "they weren't that keen to offer these brokers a better deal than they were giving their existing tied agents." In fact, in some cases, Prudential wanted to change the existing agreements that Aetna had entered into, and understandably this caused bad feelings among many independent advisers. "Prudential's handling of the acquisition gave Sovereign an opportunity to attract some quality advisers very early in the piece, which we did by offering them a better package, a wider product range and stronger service lines," says Whyte. Ironically, Prudential was later bought out by Colonial and in 2000, Colonial was taken over by Sovereign.

Prudential's purchase of Aetna was not the only event to upset the broker market and provide Sovereign with a business opportunity. Capital Life had been acquired by NZI and Royal Insurance by Sun Alliance. All of the companies taken over had relied on independent advisors and all the acquiring companies had sales forces of tied agents. "This activity caused a lot of confusion among brokers because they didn't know what was happening to them," says Hendry. The turmoil was not helped by the move to a de-regulated market. "There was a total lack of regulation and statutory requirements." Whyte recalls. "It was like the Wild West." This worked to Sovereign's advantage because the managers of established companies were accustomed to working in a highly controlled, regulated and static environment where they had the upper hand over brokers and agents alike. Hendry, on the other hand, having worked for 25 years with independent brokers both in the U.K. and Hong Kong, understood what they needed. "They are independent business people," he explains, "and they want to be respected as professional advisers. They want to be given service, they want to be given support and they want to be given the type of products they feel their clients need. None of that was recognised by any other company and so immediately there was an obvious difference in strategy between what we were doing and what other companies were doing. We developed an immediate affinity with the New Zealand broker."

Sovereign opened for business in January of 1989 and Uganecz launched the second prong of Sovereign's strategy, Caledonian Financial Services, the following month with the intention, according to Uganecz, "of delivering efficient and innovative solutions by employing the latest technologies and skilled sales people." His first staff member was Judy Hamilton who was hired as Caledonian's office manager, and who is still with Sovereign. Hamilton had been working at Hurstmere Brokers and she had got to know Coon and Hendry on their frequent visits to Hurstmere's offices.

"An expression we heard a lot was, 'a breath of fresh air'."

Having established an administrative unit, Uganecz's next challenge was to attract brokers. Initially he designed a large advertisement, which cost $1600 to place in the local paper. It drew only two responses. Extremely disappointed at the lack of response, and realising that he had a lot to learn about the New Zealand marketplace, he looked for other advertising ideas. He found a small advertisement in a book of 'best ads'. This one cost only $86 to place in the local papers and produced over 50 replies. After sorting and interviews, this translated into two brokers hired, and by June of that year, Uganecz had four brokers on his team.

Uganecz's third challenge was to convince people that the Caledonian brokers were actually *independent* financial advisers in spite of the fact Caledonian was a wholly owned subsidiary of Sovereign. In one sense they were, because Coon and Hendry always maintained that Caledonian brokers should be free to recommend whatever they considered to be the best product for their clients, irrespective of which insurance company offered them. They were convinced that Sovereign's products would compare favourably with those of their competitors. Moreover, they believed the competition would be good for Sovereign, as it would keep them on their toes. On the other hand, Caledonian brokers were biased towards Sovereign's products because they got paid a higher commission for selling these products than those of competitors. Uganecz and his successors were successful in developing Caledonian as a separate brand, and although people in the industry saw Caledonian as being an extension of Sovereign, the general public saw Caledonian advisers as being independent.

Coon and Hendry knew their strategy of providing brand new products at attractive prices and backed by first class service was the right one even by the time New Zealand had returned from its summer holidays. As the 1989 business year got under way, Sovereign came flying out of the starting blocks and raced towards its sales targets. A large number of agents were excited by the Sovereign product range and recommended them enthusiastically to their customers. Coon's vision continued to capture people's imagination. "We had a lot of naive missionaries in those days," says Uganecz with a laugh. Advisors were impressed not only with Sovereign's products, but with the way the company dealt with them. Sovereign kept the promises it made, and was friendly, fast and easy to deal with. Moreover, it was clearly market driven, always keen to respond to what its customers, the advisors themselves, wanted. Sovereign quickly became recognised as a company that excelled in marketing and that gave the advisors confidence to recommend Sovereign's products. "An expression we heard a lot was, 'a breath of fresh air'," Uganecz adds.

Hendry was not shy about advertising Sovereign's success. The first page of the company's first annual report in March of 1990, for example, has a picture of lightning coming down from a black thunderous sky with the words: "Before January 1989, the New Zealand life assurance marketplace lingered in the 'Dark Ages.' Innovation was lacking. Internationally proven products and concepts were not available to the New Zealand consumer." The reader turns the page to find a reddish orange photo of a glorious sunrise and the words: "In January 1989, the darkness ended." Sovereign later got a letter from the Northland Lightning Society congratulating them on using a picture of lightning but pointing out they had the picture upside down! Still, the company did have things to crow about. Uganecz's target had been to have 29 brokers in place by the end of 1989, and by December he had hired 27. By then, Caledonian brokers were writing approximately 40 proposals per month with a premium income to Sovereign of $50,000 to $60,000. This was less than Uganecz, Coon and Hendry had hoped for, but a useful contribution to Sovereign's business nevertheless. In the month of June, 1989, six months after opening its doors, Sovereign received over 500 proposals with an annualised premium of $850,000. By Sovereign's own estimates, only five of the 60+ companies authorised to sell life insurance in New Zealand would have written more business in that month. In August, Sovereign broke the $1 million dollar mark in new annualised premium for the first time, and then did it again in September. In its first year of operation, Sovereign wrote over $10 million worth of business. It also had assets of $6.5 million and by March 1990 had produced an operating profit of $680,000 with a further 'embedded' profit of $2 million, bringing the total profit figure to $2.8 million. In addition, Sovereign had developed six products, launched Caledonian Financial Services, built a network of independent financial advisers, recruited a management team and developed a set of operating systems powerful enough to cope with the rapid influx of business.

Hearing about Sovereign's spectacular early success, someone once asked Coon, Hendry and Uganecz whether there was ever a time when they had doubts about Sovereign's survival. "Oh, yes!" boomed Hendry, and the room erupted with laughter.

CHAPTER 8

The backlash

"At times it seemed like there were more people employed to put us out of business than we employed to run our business."

At first, Sovereign's competitors were amused at the success the upstart seemed to be having and they knew it could not last. Sovereign was seen as being a joke ("Did you hear the one about the Englishman, Scotsman and Canadian who came to New Zealand to start a life company?") and the company was dismissed as being a flash in the pan. Sovereign, they believed, was attracting interest because it was novel, and they were convinced it would soon fade into obscurity. Even the reaction of the industry organisation, the Life Offices Association, was of total disinterest. "We applied to join the LOA and they merrily accepted us as a very small niche player who was not going to write much business and who could be totally ignored," Coon recalls. Then, as the company's success continued and because they did not understand the arrangements Coon had made with the re-insurance companies, Sovereign's competitors were delighted at its rapid growth; mistakenly believing that since insurance companies lose money on every new policy sold, rapid success would be the young company's death knell. But contrary to what its competitors thought, Sovereign was there for the long haul. With the financial reassurance backing of global insurance companies such as Cologne Re and Gerling Globale, Sovereign thrived on the volume of new business it was writing. Its relationship with Eagle Star gave it credibility in the insurance world, and its association with some of the leading international fund managers ensured its success in the investment field.

But when Sovereign did not implode under the weight of its success, the upstart company moved from being a joke to being a threat. "We dominated the opposition to such an extent," says David Whyte, "that other companies felt they were under attack and they started to fight back." The first step was to mount a disinformation campaign aimed at discrediting both Sovereign and its founders. Some of Sovereign's competitors genuinely believed that Coon and Hendry were fly-by-night operators who would con both brokers and consumers out of millions of dollars and then flee the market, but others were more mischievous and, although they knew better, it suited them to promote such views. In either case, in the early years there was no shortage of rumours about Sovereign in the market place. "There were all sorts of dire predictions that Sovereign would fold within six months, six weeks or ten minutes," David Whyte recalls. Hendry nods agreement, "Many companies took the view that we had no substance, no financial strength and no future. They would tell brokers 'If you want to get involved with them that's fine but you'll look silly in a few months because they'll be gone.'" On one occasion, Coon went to a meeting with brokers and was greeted with someone saying: "I thought you were dead!"

> **Rumours about Sovereign in the early years**
> - Sovereign is run by two escaped convicts from the UK who work out of an attic.
> - Sovereign is about to be bought by (insert name of preferred company).
> - Chris Coon was being pursued by the Justice Department.(In fact he had been a consultant to the Justice department.)
> - Sovereign is run out of a basement in Takapuna which has barred windows.
> - Nobody could make any money at the rates Sovereign was charging.(In fact, in 1990 industry rates were significantly higher than today.)
> - Sovereign is financed by the Mafia.
> - The Securities Commission is going to close Sovereign on (insert preferred date here). This was particularly hard to refute because it had an element of truth to it.
> - Sovereign is broke and Coon and Hendry are about to flee the country.
> - Coon and Hendry offered to sell to Sun Alliance but they refused to touch it.

There is absolutely no doubt in the minds of anyone connected with Sovereign, and with many outside Sovereign who were active in the life insurance industry at the time, that the rumours were spread by managers at some of New Zealand's largest and most established life companies. "We believe that one or more meetings of four prominent

Wellington life offices took place to plot Sovereign's removal," says Coon. "We knew who most of the four were and thereafter referred to them as the Wellington Mafia." Dwight Whitney, Sovereign's marketing consultant, recalls that he was at a dinner party one night in 1989 and met a man boasting he had been hired by one of the established companies to lead the Sovereign dirty tricks campaign.

> *"During the first four years, there were more people employed in the industry trying to find ways of discrediting Sovereign than we employed developing our own business."*

Coon knows that one of Sovereign's reassurers met with the actuary at a leading life company who said that Sovereign was a disaster for the insurance industry and they had to do something about it. When he returned from his meeting in Wellington, the reassurer told Coon, "They don't like you down there." Shortly afterwards, Coon and Hendry were summoned to a hearing in Wellington by the Securities Commission. But Coon, ever the gentleman, puts the rumour-mongering down to ignorance rather than malice: "It comes from the arrogance of these people. They didn't believe that anyone outside their own organisation could be capable of doing things they weren't doing, and we were doing things differently. They were not aware of our reassurance arrangements so they thought we would fall over very quickly. They didn't appreciate the kind of support we were getting." The rumours were troublesome and frustrating but they had no real impact on Sovereign's continued growth. In fact, the focus on Sovereign and the misinformation campaign may have distracted key managers in competing life companies from focusing on their business. "I am sure that at various times during the first four years, there were more people employed in the industry trying to find ways of discrediting Sovereign than we employed developing our own business," Hendry muses.

But the battle was to heat up. As Sovereign became increasingly successful in snatching new business from under the establishment's noses, Sovereign's competitors took their counterattack to a new level, trying to accomplish in the back rooms through the Old Boy networks what they could not do in the market place. In fact, it was shortly after the first midyear results came out that Sovereign's legal problems began. "I can't prove it," said the late Bruce Bornholdt, Sovereign's former chairman who represented the company at their first hearings with the Securities Commission, "but I know someone in a competing company complained to the Securities Commission in 1989 and later to the Commerce Commission." Coon agrees. "The actions of the Securities Commission and all the other government bodies have been a reaction to complaints by our competitors. We don't believe there has ever been a complaint from the public."

War was declared in November of 1989. The Securities Commission wrote to Coon and Hendry accusing Sovereign of being in breach of the Securities Act and inviting them to attend a meeting in Wellington December 20th to discuss their case. The Commission took this action because they believed that all of Sovereign's products were investment products not life policies. If this was the case, they could not be offered for sale without a prospectus. "That would have killed our business," says Hendry. "It would have meant that independent advisers could not have sold our products in the normal way and we would have had to close our doors." The Commission also had concerns about some of the claims Sovereign was making in both its product advertising and the company profile.

In hindsight, Coon and Hendry both realise they took the whole situation too lightly. At the beginning, they did not understand the gravity of the situation and it was only as the process started to evolve that they realised how much trouble they were in. "In fact," says Hendry, "we just filed their first letter, thinking to ourselves, who are these guys to question our business? It is only when we got the second letter that we started to take it seriously." Even then Coon and Hendry did not realise the far-reaching consequences that the Commission's interest in Sovereign could have, and therefore they were unconcerned about the summons to appear before them. They knew that the products Sovereign offered were acceptable life insurance products overseas, and that what they were saying about both their products and themselves was also accepted industry practice elsewhere. As a result, Coon and Hendry believed a low-key meeting with the Commission would sort things out. "I was quite confident because I thought they would be like the UK Department of Trade," says Coon, causing everyone within earshot to burst out laughing. "I thought they would be knowledgeable, reasonable and fair."

Just how precarious their situation was began to dawn on Coon and Hendry while they were having lunch with their marketing consultants, Dwight Whitney and Kaye Coyne. Over lunch, Coon casually mentioned they had received a letter from the Commission and how interesting it would be to meet with the industry regulators. Coyne, who had had considerable corporate experience in New Zealand with Marac Finance, which had had its own problems with the Commission, pricked her ears up. "I don't think you're being invited to have tea with the Securities Commission," she said, alarmed at their naiveté. Coyne then proceeded to outline what could happen and what steps they should take to protect themselves and their new company.

> "I don't think you're being invited to have tea with the Securities Commission."

Once they realised the full implications of the hearing, Coon and Hendry decided they would meet the Securities Commission head on and mount a strong defence. Coyne gave them the name of a QC who might have been able to assist them, but he declined due to a conflict of interest. As it turned out, he did them an immense favour by recommending Bruce Bornholdt, a seasoned and well-connected commercial lawyer who had been the first chairman of the Commerce Commission when it had been established by the Labour Government in 1975. The craggy-faced Bornholdt whose blue eyes would twinkle with delight when he recalled his battles with the Commission was, by his own admission, a street fighter. Hendry agrees with Bornholdt's view of himself. "It was so strange," he says, "Bruce was one of the nicest guys you would ever want to meet but in the courtroom, he was the most aggressive lawyer I have ever seen."

Bornholdt had a simple strategy: prepare thoroughly, go in confidently, dominate and look for trade-offs. The day before the hearing, Ian, Chris and their solicitor, Eric Bachmann of Hesketh Henry, met Bornholdt in his Wellington chambers for the first of what was to be many long gruelling sessions. Bornholdt had to be educated by Hendry and Coon as to how the life industry worked and, for his part, he had to convince the passionate entrepreneurs to temper their marketing material. During this time, Bachmann laboured incessantly drawing up the legal papers Bruce wanted available so he could overwhelm the Commission. This first meeting with the Commission also began a new life-long career for Bachmann, which everyone jokingly refers to as 'keeping Ian out of jail'. To this day, all of Sovereign's marketing material has to be reviewed by this quiet bookish solicitor because, as Hendry now admits, "We made some pretty outrageous claims in those days!" Today, Sovereign's marketing material is a little more subdued although Bachmann still has his challenges. "The marketing staff never tire of trying to slip one past me," he says with a wry smile.

In Wellington, Sovereign faced an uphill battle. The late Colin Paterson, a Wellington commercial lawyer, who was well known for his independent and often extreme views, chaired the Securities Commission. Moreover, the chief executive officer of the Commission was, and still is, John Farrell. Farrell believed strongly that government regulation was necessary to prevent the public from being exploited by large commercial corporations. The Commission's principal investigator, Kerry Morrell, was particularly difficult. "He was a real nit-picker," recalled Bornholdt. "He wanted every i dotted and every t crossed."

On December 20th at 2PM on a pleasant summer's afternoon, Coon, Hendry, Bachmann and Bornholdt arrived for the meeting in the Commission's offices in Greenock House on The Terrace in Wellington. The meeting room was very large with a big oval table in the centre and windows along two sides. Everyone sat round the table with the Commission members and staff along one side and the Sovereign team along the other. "It was a bit disappointing," says Ian. "The room was not set up for a formal hearing and it wasn't very imposing. Here we were on trial for our lives in very ordinary surroundings!" The proceedings were opened by the chairman, Colin Paterson, a small, thin man with grey hair, sharp prominent features and glasses. Paterson was an astute commercial lawyer who had guided large corporations like Shell New Zealand through troubled waters such as the government investigation into the oil industry. He had a reputation for having a keen mind and a very combative, some would say, offensive, nature. With his customary directness he began the hearing without introducing any of the Commission members or their staff, getting instead straight to the charges against Sovereign. Once Paterson had had his say, he turned it over to Coon and Hendry saying in effect, "Well, what have you got to say for yourselves?"

As it turned out, Bornholdt had a lot to say. He quickly tried to gain the upper hand by forcefully defending Sovereign and by attacking the Commission's position. Bornholdt had a number of written submissions he wished to put before the Commission and his first battle was to get Paterson to agree to them being introduced. Initially this was refused but Bornholdt persevered and, eventually, Paterson allowed them to be presented. Coon then made a statement describing Sovereign's products and how such products are commonly used overseas. After this brief presentation there was a period of questioning, dominated by Paterson, which on reflection Coon and Hendry admit they could have handled better. "We kept talking about accepted practice in the U.K. and the commissioners kept saying, 'We don't care about the United Kingdom. This is New Zealand,' " says Hendry ruefully. The hearing was short but stormy with Paterson and Bornholdt, who are both fond of talking, struggling to dominate and Coon and Hendry trying to educate both of them about accepted life industry practices in New Zealand and overseas. As Hendry remembers it, Paterson would frequently interrupt them before they could finish answering his questions. "It was a Kangaroo Court," he says contemptuously, "and, it would have been funny except we were on trial for our lives." But not everyone found the meeting stressful. None of Paterson's fellow Commissioners said a word and one even fell asleep part way through the meeting!

One hour after it had started, Paterson brought the hearing to a close. Without consulting any of the other Commissioners, he made an order directing Sovereign to stop selling one of its products, the Guaranteed Income Plan, immediately. "It was as if he wanted his pound of flesh," says Hendry. "It didn't matter what points we raised, they were going to do something to try to stop us because they believed we were a bunch of crooks." After making the order, Paterson adjourned the meeting until January so the Securities Commission could extend its examination into Sovereign's other business practices. Paterson and his fellow commissioners then left the room and afternoon tea was brought in for the defendants and any of the Commission staff who chose to stay and make polite conversation.

The order Paterson made was relatively mild and had little real impact on Sovereign's day-to-day operation. The Guaranteed Income Policy had not been well received in the New Zealand marketplace and Coon and Hendry were contemplating withdrawing it anyway. The question is, why did Paterson, who seemed determined to put Sovereign out of business, back down in the end? Coon, Hendry and their legal advisers believe that Paterson had a predetermined course of action he intended to follow in the hearing but was stopped when Sovereign put up such a strong defence, a defence which was legally sound and strenuously argued. "The Commission was surprised that we defended ourselves," says Hendry. "They expected we would be like lambs to the slaughter." Bornholdt agreed. "I think Paterson realised we might go off half-cocked if he acted strongly. I think he was afraid we would ask for a judicial review." The fact that Paterson made any order at all was possibly a face saving gesture as much as anything else.

Although Sovereign emerged from the first battle with only minor wounds, the war was to escalate and would be fought on a number of other fronts. The scheduled January meeting was not to be, however. Throughout the December meeting, Paterson chain-smoked and coughed constantly. "He did not look well," Coon recalls. "I thought to myself, you're not long for this world, my friend." Two weeks later Paterson was dead. The January hearing was postponed until March and under a new chairman the meetings were more structured and less confrontational. The scope of the Commission's inquiry was broadened to include all of Sovereign's marketing activity and then, not understanding Sovereign's arrangements with its reassurers, the Commission questioned the company's solvency. "The whole thing started out as being relatively minor," says Hendry. "But after being assured our products were legitimate life insurance products, they broadened their investigation into the financial structure of Sovereign. They had clearly decided Chris and I were not the sort of people they wanted working in the life industry in New Zealand." Many of the meetings with the Securities Commission were life and death situations for Sovereign as the Commission repeatedly threatened to make orders that would have had the effect of closing the company down. On one occasion, Sovereign was so close to being closed that its lawyers prepared a defence to the Commission and at the same time an application for an injunction to the High Court staying the Commission's expected order. Some of the lawyers involved in Sovereign's defence were not optimistic about the success of either and refused to work on the case unless their fees were paid in advance.

> *None of Paterson's fellow Commissioners said3 a word and one even fell asleep part way through the meeting!*

Dealing with the Securities Commission became an exercise first in overcoming the Commissioners' preconceived ideas that Hendry and Coon appeared to be cowboys and crooks determined to defraud New Zealand consumers, and second, in educating them about the life industry. This was not an easy task given their preconceived ideas about Sovereign. On one occasion, Coon recalls, the Registrar of Companies and Government Actuary told them, "I don't know anything about your company but I don't like it." On another, a member of the Commission said, "I'm not a tax expert but I think you're wrong about your tax arrangements." These were incredible things to say to a man like Coon who has years of experience with taxation in the life industry. At the conclusion of the hearings Coon and Hendry were completely shattered. They found many of the Commission's questions hard to understand. "It was very frustrating being judged by people who knew very little about our industry," says Hendry. Bornholdt continued with his successful strategy of being very well prepared and taking the offensive by bombarding the Commission with paperwork. "I think they were always surprised at how well prepared we were," he recalled with a laugh.

> *"They had decided Chris and I were not the sort of people they wanted working in the life industry in New Zealand."*

The first battle, which began in November of 1989, ended in March of 1991 when the Securities Commission granted Sovereign a new letter of authorisation allowing them to operate as a life company. The turning point in the life and death struggle came only when Sovereign arranged for Dr Norbert Pyhel, one of the most respected executives in the re-insurance industry, to appear before the Commission to explain how reassurance worked, what his company's arrangements were with Sovereign and why he chose to do business with Coon and Hendry. Pyhel's visit impressed the Commission although the commissioners had trouble understanding why some of the world's leading reassurers would do business with an upstart company like Sovereign. They simply did not realise the reputation Coon had overseas. "What they couldn't believe," says Coon, "is that three of the largest reassurers in the world would want to do business with a company like Sovereign when they could have been involved with AMP and National Mutual." After that meeting, the Commission dropped the issue of solvency. But the war was far from over. The Securities Commission has retained an active interest in Sovereign throughout the past 12 years, especially between 1991 and 1998 when Sovereign was required to answer to the Securities Commission or the Commerce Commission more times than anyone can remember. For example, there was a fracas with the

Commerce Commission in 1995," recalls Bachmann. "They did a covert investigation of one of our brokers and the *Home Plan 1000* product. Two officers pretended to be prospective purchasers. It took eight months to resolve all their concerns."

The war with the Securities Commission has been a very costly affair for Sovereign. Not only has the financial cost been in the millions of dollars, but it has also taken thousands of hours of senior executive time and energy. During the first battle in 1989-1991, Hendry estimates that ten per cent of his time and even a greater share of Coon's time was spent preparing for Securities Commission hearings. "And the amount of time spent worrying was much greater," he adds wistfully. Coon and Hendry carried the burden of the fight for survival themselves because they wanted the staff to remain focused on building the company. They were successful. "During our second year, Sovereign could have been shut down at any moment," says Ballantyne. "But most of us didn't realise that because Chris and Ian protected us from it." Thus, for the staff it was business as usual during this stressful period.

At Sovereign, business as usual means only one thing. Rapid growth.

CHAPTER 9

Business as usual

"I have never been discouraged by mistakes. I don't expect people to be 100% right, but I do expect them to help."

Sovereign's second year continued to be a time of excellent growth. "Despite the economic recession, and increased competition in the life assurance market, Sovereign grew rapidly, and continued to set new standards in the life assurance and investment sectors," says Coon. During this time, Sovereign's market share increased, as did staff numbers and the size of the board of directors. Three new products were launched, and the marketing of existing products was expanded. The network of independent financial advisers and brokers who were selling Sovereign's products continued to grow, and new systems were developed to improve the level of service to both these brokers and to Sovereign policyholders. Sovereign's staff increased at the rate of seven or eight new people every three months. The company maintained its profitability with an operating profit of $332,600, a good return considering the investment made in people, systems and marketing during the year. New annualised premium increased 28% to $10.2 million and single premiums increased a whopping 60% to $4.2 million. As a result, net tangible assets grew to $12.2 million and the company's capital base grew from $2 million to $5 million. Sovereign's managed funds continued to be outstanding performers.

Sovereign's success in the marketplace resulted from Coon's product ideas and Hendry's success in building an effective organisation. Experience had taught Hendry that a company is only as good as its people and, that at the end of the day, someone's attitude and ability was more important than their age and experience. Consequently, when he recruited staff, Hendry did not make the mistake so many companies make of hiring people who did not share the company vision and values. Hendry also understood that how individuals perform is greatly influenced by the culture of the organisation. He knew that the vision and values of Sovereign's senior managers, the standards and policies they set, and the systems and processes they developed would all affect what people would focus on, how motivated they would be to achieve their goals, the quality of their work, and how they would behave towards both each other and their customers. "People have to have jobs they enjoy," says Hendry. "You have to create the right environment and you have to develop people so they can grow with the company."

The wellspring of Sovereign's success-orientated culture is the partnership between Coon and Hendry. Both are optimistic, confident and energetic people. They do not posture and try to impress. Neither has a large ego. They just have complete faith in their ideas and their abilities. Like nearly all successful entrepreneurs, it never occurred to them that they might fail. This positive attitude lead to an belief among each of the company's early employees that Sovereign was small but right. They realised Sovereign was the underdog but they just knew the company would succeed. Coon and Hendry are also very hard working and fiercely competitive, motivated not by wealth, fame or status, but by the desire to succeed. Hendry played bowls competitively and was a top ranked player in his club. Coon likewise is very competitive. Once, at a team building session for senior managers, each person was asked what they would like to accomplish in the next twelve months. The IT manager wanted to improve his systems, the sales manager aimed for larger market share and the operations manager strove for performance improvement. Coon's goal was to annihilate the competition. Again this attitude became part of the Sovereign culture. Sovereign's staff were not just out to challenge the establishment. They were out to win.

The success of Coon and Hendry's partnership is due partly to their shared vision and partly to the clear division of responsibility between them. "We both know

"It was a great environment to work in. The entrepreneurial spirit abounded."

what we like doing and what we don't like doing," says Hendry. "Chris likes doing his financial engineering, he likes doing the actuarial side of it, the product design - and he is superb in those areas. I like the marketing side of it. I like developing the business, and the cut and thrust of competition." This understanding has meant that there have been no 'turf wars' between the two, no rivalries of any kind. They respect each other's expertise and there is a high level of trust between them. Disagreements, which are rare, are discussions never arguments. They are very supportive of each other and very accepting of each other's weaknesses. Anyone who has worked closely with senior executives will recognise that this is an exceptional business relationship.

The culture Coon and Hendry wanted for Sovereign was that of an entrepreneurial company, customer driven, challenging, innovative, and experimental. They wanted Sovereign to be a place where decisions were made quickly, and they were successful. "It was a great environment to work in," remembers David Whyte. "The entrepreneurial spirit abounded. Sovereign was a flat organisation and you were given free reign to get on with your job. Errors were not frowned upon or seriously criticised, you were encouraged to do what you thought best." Both Coon and Hendry have an 'entrepreneurial flair' themselves even though both were brought up to, in Coon's words, 'slot into a neat little institutional role where you don't actually stray into an entrepreneurial position.' But their nature has always been to question and to challenge. Neither will accept something simply because it has always been that way. Because the emphasis was on self-improvement, process development and innovation, Coon and Hendry's tolerance for risk taking and mistakes was high. "I've never been discouraged by mistakes," says Coon. "I don't expect people to be one hundred percent right, but I do expect them to help." Like most successful people, Coon and Hendry both have the ability to learn from mistakes but then quickly put those mistakes behind them. Successes, on the other hand, can nourish them for a long time.

On a personal level, both Coon and Hendry are friendly, down to earth and approachable. As a result, in the early days, the Sovereign culture was one of informality and teamwork. There was no hierarchy and no protocol. "You could just walk into Chris or Ian's office at any time and ask them questions about anything and they always had time to answer your questions," says Ballantyne. Even today, Sovereign is a people-orientated company where staff are valued and treated well. Most staff describe Sovereign as a fun place to work and early staff remember fondly the informality, comradeship and fun than existed. "Everyone threw themselves into their work. We set champagne targets and then would work very long hours to break them," recalls Russell Hutchinson, who was Sovereign's marketing manager until 1999. "Then we would socialise together on Friday afternoons after work, or playing sport together." Lyn Dorreen was hired by Sovereign in August of 1990 to develop a new filing system. She arrived to find files just stacked in piles on the floor. Doreen describes the culture of Sovereign in those days as being one of camaraderie and teamwork. "We were just one big team," she says. "We had weekly team meetings at work and we did a lot of socialising together outside of work hours. One year, Chris even played a season of touch rugby on the staff team!"

Long before the idea became popular, Coon and Hendry believed that if you looked after your staff, they would look after the customers. "Ian and Chris have always been generous employers," says Ballantyne. "They have provided staff with rewards, share options, profit sharing, staff Christmas parties, children's Christmas parties, a staff cafeteria, a gym, mid-year staff functions, funding for Sovereign sports teams and sponsorship for individual staff who excelled in their sporting or cultural fields. When we were smaller, Ian and Chris each had the entire staff come to their homes." The philosophy at Sovereign has always been to treat people as responsible adults. For example, Sovereign rarely pays staff overtime, but people are free to take time off whenever they need it. "Our belief is that if you look after your people well," says Ballantyne, "you will get it back many-fold. It is not the dollar value that matters," she adds. "People appreciate the gesture." Doreen agrees. "The staff is very well looked after at Sovereign. We have staff functions involving partners, a group medical scheme, group life insurance, car parks, and sponsored sports teams. The staff really appreciates it, too. People work hard and are loyal to the company because they are proud to work at Sovereign."

> *Coon and Hendry believed that if you looked after your staff, they would look after the customers.*

Russell Hutchinson joined the company in August of 1989. He had been with Aetna but after they were bought out by Prudential, a broker suggested he apply to Sovereign. His first job at Sovereign was to write commission cheques, by hand! Hutchinson's role rapidly grew and he was soon involved in gathering information about Sovereign's competitors and working closely with brokers. Later he worked with Hendry in the development of marketing materials and eventually became responsible for Sovereign's marketing activity. When Hutchinson joined Sovereign, there were 15 employees and he was given a three-foot desk right outside Hendry's office. "It was a small company in those days," Hutchinson recalls. "You knew everything about what was going on in the company so everyone just did whatever had to be done to make the place run." Doreen remembers it that way, too. "It was really small back then," she says. "You knew everyone else and there was a great team environment. Everybody was friendly and open, and they all wanted to do the same thing: look after the customer. Even today we have regular team meetings to see how we can help each other."

Coon and Hendry have both taken pride in the way staff have made Sovereign a focal point of their lives. "At the moment people are working hard during the day," Hendry said in an interview in 1992, "but on Monday nights many of our staff are at Dragon Boat practice. On Tuesday, many of them work late; Wednesday a lot of them are involved in netball; Thursday a number of people including Chris play Touch Rugby for the company and on Friday they stay in the office when we have our little social get-together. If you come in over the weekend you usually find a couple of people in the office. So there is a life outside of Sovereign but for a lot of people, a lot of what they do is connected to Sovereign in some way." Coon agreed. "And I think that has helped the success of the company," he added.

> *"It was a young dynamic company full of imaginative people not afraid to take risks."*

Although it is very supportive, Sovereign's culture is also one of demanding standards and high performance. Both Coon and Hendry have very high ideals, especially about business morality and work performance. "The way Sovereign operates is the way we personally do business," says Coon. "It is our sense of honesty, fairness and integrity that drives the company." These are not just empty words. When Coon was with Liberty Life, for example, he negotiated a re-insurance arrangement with Gerling, a German reassurance company that resulted in Gerling investing substantially in Liberty. At the time the investment was made, the exchange rate was 12 marks to the pound. But when the time came for Gerling to be repaid, the exchange rate had dropped to only 4 marks to the pound, effectively reducing Gerling's profit by 67%. "Gerling's investment had helped Liberty grow from being worth zilch to something like 50-60 million pounds," says Coon. "So, I felt we were honour bound to protect them from their currency loss." Gerling's executives were impressed with Coon's morality and, when they learned that he planned to start a new life company in New Zealand, they told him they would like to be his lead reassurer.

Most employees who joined Sovereign prior to 1995 did so because of Coon and Hendry, and their vision of an innovative customer-focused, high performing company. Ian Perry, who has his doctorate in Geology and has held a number of middle management positions since joining Sovereign, is typical of that group. A friend told him about Sovereign and he came to have a look around. Perry was impressed with what he saw but it was his interview with Hendry that convinced him to accept a position. "I bought the man not the company," he says. "I saw a man who knew how to run a company. He was in touch with everything that was going on and he had a clear vision of where he wanted to go." Several years later, Perry feels the same way. "This is still a company I want to work for because of Ian and Chris. I have confidence in their partnership." Errol Timmins, Sovereign's underwriter, agrees. Timmins joined Sovereign in 1990 at the age of 23, after spending four years with AMP. Like Ballantyne, he was attracted to Sovereign because it was the antithesis of the traditional insurance companies. "Sovereign had all the things I liked as an employer and as an insurance company," says Timmins. "It was a young dynamic company full of imaginative people not afraid to take risks; whereas AMP was declining and obsessed with cost cutting." Sovereign's small size also appealed. "Chris and Ian were very accessible," he says. "You were never more than a couple of steps away from the man who made the decisions." Timmins particularly liked the way everyone pitched in to do whatever had to be done. "You had to be very multi-skilled back then," he adds.

More than anything else, Sovereign's culture was driven by Coon and Hendry's view of putting the customers first, a concept enthusiastically advocated by Ballantyne. They knew that although efficiency was important, being flexible enough to meet the customer's needs was paramount. Because Coon and Hendry hired only those people who shared their values, it was easy to build a customer driven business. Each person knew the rule was to do whatever was necessary to make the customer not just happy, but also successful. "We would do anything to put the customer first," recalls Perry. "Even if we had to upset our standard operating procedures, we would do anything to help the customer. We never said 'no' outright." Doreen agrees. "We were always trying to find ways of doing what the customer wanted." They usually succeeded. "Working with Sovereign was very personal. Right from the start you had the feeling that nothing was too much trouble. Everyone was very friendly and very approachable," says Judy Hamilton, who as Caledonian Financial Services office manager, worked closely with Sovereign staff.

Hendry's management style was to hire the right people, give them the tools they needed to do their jobs, and then get out of their way so they could get on with it. This was a style that suited Ballantyne. During her 12 years at Sovereign, she was known as the 'Custodian of the Culture.' From the outset, she took it upon herself to promote, develop and guard the service culture that defines Sovereign. "Naomi was a very strong communicator and she was absolutely passionate about the Sovereign vision," says Timmins. "She would pull people together and pound the pulpit. She was very charismatic." Doreen agrees. "Naomi was the most influential person around here. People could see she was passionate about Sovereign becoming a world-class company; about us doing the right thing; and about acting with honesty and integrity. Just how effective a leader she was became apparent in 1990 when Ballantyne went on maternity leave for nine months. "While she was away performance slipped, inefficiencies crept in and people became unhappy," says Timmins. "Naomi came back, called everyone together, shook the tree and demanded better results." Hutchinson remembers that time, too. "The spirit of the place really declined while Naomi was away," he says. "We appreciated her value and the way she focused us on the action that was required."

Ballantyne's goal was to create a culture based on customer service, high performance, individual accountability and teamwork. "My role was to encourage people to take responsibility, to make decisions and to use their initiative," says Ballantyne. "I was there to give assistance, to show people the process and to be a problem solving resource. But they are closest to the action and so they are the only ones who can make it happen." Timmins was one of many who appreciated that approach. "You were given the freedom to make decisions relating to your own job," he recalls. "But with that freedom went the accountability. This was in marked contrast to AMP." Like Hendry, Ballantyne had very high standards and was quick to deal with what she considered to be performance problems. On one occasion, she had a problem with two of her team leaders. One was married and the other engaged but they developed a relationship, which began on a company team-building weekend. Eventually their relationship caused problems for their teams at work. Ballantyne took them aside and offered them the choice of taking a demotion or resigning. If they chose to stay, she promised to provide counselling for them and their partners. The man left but the woman stayed with Sovereign. Today, she has worked her way back to being a manager. "I got criticised by some people for making moral judgements," says Ballantyne. "But I felt I had to deal with the situation to protect the staff and the company." Ballantyne was as quick to give recognition for work well done, as she was to criticise. She constantly talked about her expectations, her values and her goals for her department. She put performance plans in place for each member of her staff so they could see their potential future development. As a result, she gained the loyalty of her direct reports. Her team (there were 30 employees by the end of 1990, and 200 by the time she left Sovereign in 2001) became a strong unit that worked long hours and then socialised together after work. "We all looked after each other in those days," says Hutchinson. "We were a really close knit team." Timmins agrees. "There was tremendous team spirit which was driven by Naomi," he says. "People loved their work and took pride in it. They could see the growth of the company and the success we were having. They could also see that they were benefiting from it."

Due to its rapid growth, by late 1989, Sovereign had outgrown its premises. Coon and Hendry leased temporary additional space at 15 Anzac Street and moved their broker development and mortgage sections there. At the same time, the decision was made to move Sovereign's Head Office into a new commercial complex being built by ASB Bank on Hurstmere Road in the central business district of Takapuna. "Chris and Ian wanted to make sure that everyone had a pleasant working environment," says Hutchinson. "That reflects their total quality approach to the organisation." The building was scheduled to be completed in June of 1990 but in the end, was not ready until October. But once they had moved in, Sovereign's growth was so great that it did not take them long to fill up the entire third floor.

In Sovereign's second year of operation, Coon and Hendry stayed with their business strategy of both building a network of independent financial advisers throughout New Zealand, and establishing their own brokerage through Caledonian Financial Services. The second year was tough for Caledonian. Many of the original advisers left, causing business to be lost. Part of the problem was that Uganecz had recruited too many sales managers who, because they were unaccustomed to working in a open market, had difficulty recruiting and retaining advisers. By the middle of 1990, Coon and Hendry decided that Uganecz should take on a different role within Sovereign and Daryl McAlinden, who had been recruited from Colonial Mutual to be broker training manager with Sovereign, became Caledonian's managing director. McAlinden managed the change in leadership effectively and all of the advisers Uganecz had recruited stayed with Caledonian as a result. He then set about lifting their performance. "Daryl was very good at training and sales," says Judy Hamilton. "Caledonian hadn't really been performing in its first two years and he got it off the ground."

> *"My aim was to ensure the calibre within our organisation reflected Sovereign's commitment to professionalism, efficiency and integrity. I wanted our people to be the best."*

To ensure that the independent advisers selling its products received the level of service they deserved, Sovereign recruited more staff at all levels, and also continued to develop its systems. In 1989, Dominic Khaw was appointed company accountant. He was joined later in the year by John Lamb, Peter Rourke and Angela Eastwood. Lamb was appointed systems support manager and his primary task was to develop software for brokers and advisers. Rourke was recruited from the UK where he was a successful financial adviser, and came to New Zealand specifically to be a Sovereign broker development manager. Reflecting its commitment to its staff, Angela Eastwood was appointed personnel and human resources manager. "My aim," says Angela, "was to ensure the calibre within our organisation reflected Sovereign's commitment to professionalism, efficiency and integrity. I wanted our people to be the best." Jane Durrant came from Guardian Assurance to be finance manager, with responsibility for managing Sovereign's day-to-day financial affairs. Alan Stuart, who had been at Royal Assurance and then chief underwriter at Sun Alliance after the merger, was named new business and policy servicing manager. Stuart's strength was in disability underwriting and his appointment coincided with Sovereign's entry into the disability market. Martin Allison, an experienced specialist, was recruited as superannuation manger in line with Coon and Hendry's strategy of making superannuation a key part of Sovereign's business. Overall, Sovereign's staff continued to grow at the rate of seven people per quarter throughout its second year of operation.

In 1990, Sovereign launched *Sovereign Income Protector*. "It was our belief that the 1990s would be the disability decade," says Coon. "And we saw that income protection was the most neglected form of personal insurance in New Zealand. Given that statistics show 4 out of every 10 people face the prospect of some form of disability or illness in their lives, it was ironic this style of insurance had been a slow starter." To be consistent with their overall strategy, Coon and Hendry designed *Sovereign Income Protector* to be an investment product operating within the *Investor Plus* Balanced Growth Fund. Depending on how long the policy had been in force, clients' premiums were used to buy units in the Balanced Growth Fund with the cash allotments from the Fund being used to pay the cost of the insurance cover. Thus not only would the insured receive up to 75% of their income should they be unable to work, but at the expiry of the policy they had the potential to receive a bonus based on the performance of the investment fund. The *Sovereign Income Protector* was suitable for anyone; however, it was specifically aimed at professionals and self-employed people. There was also a special coverage for housewives, househusbands and students who are normally excluded from disability insurance because they do not earn an income. Sovereign was prepared to pay these people one thousand dollars per month should they become disabled due to accident or illness.

At the same time as *Sovereign Income Protector* was launched, *Superinvestor* and *Sovereign Variable Retirement Income* were introduced. *Superinvestor* was a personal and portable superannuation plan aimed primarily at self-employed business and professional people. Policyholders agreed to make contributions of $50 a month or more to one of Sovereign's investment funds and if they did, they would receive a lump sum payment plus a bonus of up to 4% of their contributions at the time of maturity. In keeping with Coon and Hendry's philosophy of creating flexible products, *Superinvestor* was inflation indexed, provided disability and death cover, and access to mortgage funds. The *Sovereign Variable Retirement Income* targeted people who were retired and had a lump sum they wished to invest to gain a regular income. The minimum lump sum contribution was $10,000, which was then used to buy units in one of Sovereign's investment funds. Policyholders could choose how they received their investment income from a wide range of alternatives. The *Sovereign Variable Retirement Income* was designed to encourage members of other superannuation schemes, who were just reaching retirement, to reinvest their money with Sovereign.

One of Sovereign's most successful initiatives was the *Underwriter's*

Guide, developed in 1991 as part of the company's commitment to make doing business with Sovereign easier for both the broker and the policyholder, and also more efficient for the company. "The development of the guide was driven by complaints from brokers who didn't know the rules and who couldn't manage their client's expectations," says Ballantyne. "There was a great deal of frustration all around as a result. And, underwriting had developed the reputation of being black magic." At the time, developing the guide was a very bold step. In fact it was the first such guide in Australasia and quite possibly a world-first. The guide effectively took the mystery out of the sacred insurance process that was an insurance company's method of managing its risk and controlling the sales process. Ballantyne believed that it was possible to produce a simple book that made the process of assessing risk more transparent, allowing brokers and consumers alike to understand how Sovereign measured and classified risks such as age, life-style and health. "We rang around the other insurance companies," she says, "but nobody had anything like it. We had to be careful about allowing the brokers to commit the company to bad risks but we decided that following the 80/20 rule, there must be a lot of basic issues that we could cover." Coon and Hendry supported the idea because they wanted to position Sovereign as the champion of the customer and as a company that would bring information and power to the brokers who were working directly with the policyholders. They believed that if brokers were armed with information and had the ability to make decisions in the customer's living room, they would behave more competently and look more professional. The guide was produced by a team consisting of Ballantyne, some of her staff and Sovereign's marketing consultant, Dwight Whitney. It was a huge success. "We launched it through road shows around the country," says Ballantyne. "We had a wonderful response from brokers because it was the first time that anyone had explained the underwriting process and criteria to them." The guide made a major contribution to the way life insurance was sold in New Zealand, and within months of its release, every one of Sovereign's major competitors had released its own underwriter's guide. They all looked remarkably similar to Sovereign's! Later, Sovereign made its guide available on-line.

With their eye to the future, Coon and Hendry decided to add depth and credibility to Sovereign's board of directors, which at that time consisted of Coon, Hendry and Neil Weeks, Eagle Star's representative, by recruiting outside non-executive directors. Once again, Kaye Coyne had a useful contact. At Marac, she had worked with Dennis Ferrier who was chief executive of Marac's merchant bank. Ferrier later went on to become chief executive at ASB Bank but after he retired from the ASB in 1991, Coyne suggested that he would make an excellent non-executive director. When Coon and Hendry approached Ferrier, he was very interested, however, he would make no commitment. Ferrier then spent several weeks checking on Coon and Hendry. Satisfied that he was dealing with experienced and reputable people, and that Sovereign was a sound company, he accepted the position. "I was interested in this new organisation," said Ferrier in the May 1991 issue of Sovereign Review, the company's newsletter, "because I saw Sovereign as being a great challenge with excellent long-term potential." Luring Ferrier onto the board was a coup for Sovereign. "He was a man of high intellect and big ideas. He was very demanding but he also had a great sense of humour," says Ralph Norris who reported to Ferrier at ASB Bank, and later took over as the bank's CEO. Ferrier also had a high public profile and was known for his willingness to attack the establishment. He once locked horns with Prime Minister Robert Muldoon in a bitter public debate about economic reforms. In the battle with Muldoon, Ferrier fired the final public salvo by cancelling Muldoon's ASB passbook. "Having a client like him is not good for business," he said.

"I was interested in this new organisation because I saw Sovereign as being a great challenge with excellent long-term potential."

In 1992, Bruce Bornholdt joined Ferrier on the expanded Sovereign board. Having gone into combat for the company against the Securities Commission, Bornholdt was well known to both Coon and Hendry. His standing in the legal community, as well as his experience as chairman of the Commerce Commission, made him a suitable candidate. In the same year, accountant Fred Watson was also invited to join the board to provide a more conservative bent to the group. A partner in accounting firm KPMG, Watson was perhaps best known as the Equiticorp receiver. He also sat on other prestigious boards such as Fullers, McDonald's and Waitemata Health.

At the end of its second year, Sovereign's issued and paid up capital base was increased from $2 million to $5 million. This increase was funded by Hannover Re, another of the world's leading re-insurance companies. Not only did the agreement with Hannover Re give Sovereign the working capital it needed to fund its growth, it represented a very significant endorsement of the fledgling company. Indeed, both Hannover Re's investment and Ferrier's acceptance of a board position were significant votes of confidence in Sovereign's commercial future and did a lot to reassure brokers and policyholders alike. Ferrier's appointment, especially, brought a great deal of mana and commercial experience to Sovereign.

The Securities Commission never let up. During this period of frenzied growth, Coon and Hendry had to spend large amounts of time and money, neither of which they could afford, in a fight that at any moment could cost them their company. Sovereign was experiencing phenomenal success in the marketplace and yet lived with regulatory body that could administer a lethal injection with the stroke of a pen. "At any given moment," says Hendry, "we could have lost the business."

But as Coon and Hendry were about to discover, the hand that tried to end Sovereign's life would not belong to their arch-enemy, but their best friend.

CHAPTER 10

One of our finest hours

"They knew we were in a weak position because of our rapid growth and the problems we were having with the Securities Commission." "They really put a gun to our heads. They told us they had been talking to people in Wellington and that if we didn't agree to their offer, we should be very worried."

Commerce is a social activity, and therefore the foundation for business success is laid by building relationships with key people. These people might be staff, customers, suppliers, investors or colleagues. One of the reasons Coon was able to turn his dream into reality was because he had developed strong relationships with the executives he had encountered in some of the world's top insurance and re-insurance companies. His relationship with Duncan Ferguson at Eagle Star was particularly valuable because it led to his partnership with Ian Hendry, and because it resulted in Eagle Star's Australian company agreeing to take a share holding in Sovereign. This gave the fledgling company the credibility and international connections it needed.

But relationships change and people move on, so that even before Sovereign had opened its doors in 1989, Ferguson had left Eagle Star leaving Sovereign exposed. Ferguson had been a strong and influential supporter of both Coon and Sovereign, but other Eagle Star executives did not share his enthusiasm. To make matters worse, by 1989 Sovereign had really lost two supporters in Eagle Star because Hendry, who had written the report recommending that Eagle Star become part of the new venture, had already left the company to join Coon in New Zealand. With Hendry and Ferguson gone, there was no one left within Eagle Star to support Sovereign. As a result, Eagle Star's senior management began to question whether they would honour their agreement with Coon and proceed with the proposed 25% shareholding. It was a near thing. London had decided it had no interest in New Zealand and was on the verge of withdrawing from the deal but at the last minute they decided to pass it over to Australia to make the final decision.

> "We paid a high price to get Eagle Star on board, but we needed the credibility that could only come from having an international institution owning shares in the business."

Again relationships made the difference. Eagle Star's Australian Life Division was headed by John Reid, and it was Reid who was given the job of deciding to go ahead or pull out. At this point, Sovereign was just about up and running. Fortunately, Reid had worked with Hendry in Hong Kong and so Hendry and Coon went to Sydney to see him. They were able to persuade Reid to continue with the investment and Reid, in turn, was able to persuade his board to put up the money to acquire a reduced equity stake, amounting to 9.9% of Sovereign's shares. If there had been no previous relationship between Hendry and Reid, Reid would probably not have supported the investment, and without Reid's support, the Australian board would certainly have reneged. The loss of access to Eagle Star's resources and contacts would have seriously reduced Sovereign's chances of succeeding.

Even with Reid's support, the cost of getting Eagle Star's involvement was steep. The Australians negotiated a deal that effectively gave Eagle Star majority control of Sovereign although it was only a minority shareholder. As a result, there were many things that Sovereign could not do without the approval of Eagle Star's representative. Hendry and Coon knew that it was not a good deal for Sovereign but they believed they had no choice. "We paid a high price to get them on board," Hendry admits, "but we needed the credibility that could only come from having an international institution owning shares in the business." Consequently Hendry and Coon accepted the loss of control as being the price for Eagle Star's support. But then they did not know that it would nearly cost them their company.

In 1990, the chief executive of Australian Eagle moved on and was replaced by Rodney Lester. Although Lester had run an insurance company in New Zealand much earlier in his career, he had no prior relationship with Coon, Hendry or Sovereign. He was not very positive about the investment he had inherited. As a graduate of the Harvard Business School, he had developed the view that owning 9.9% of anything was not very smart. As a result, he either wanted to get out of Sovereign or own it. With a representative on the board, Eagle Star knew exactly how Sovereign was doing, what its strengths were and also where the weaknesses lay. In addition, Eagle Star had a report from one of its actuaries in England saying that Sovereign was a potential gold mine. Lester decided to make his move and Sovereign's partner became a corporate raider.

Eagle Star realised that Sovereign's spectacular early growth created the need for more capital and that they would likely be approached to inject additional funds. Instead of supporting their business partner, Eagle Star saw Sovereign's early success as creating a vulnerability they could exploit to take over the young company at a fire sale price. "They knew we were in a weak position because of our rapid growth and the problems we were having with the Securities Commission," Hendry recalls. In fact, the Australians were adding to Sovereign's troubles by talking directly to people in Wellington saying they had concerns about Sovereign, too.

Eagle Star's management made overtures to Coon and Hendry that led them to believe the Australians were interested in increasing their stake in Sovereign. Coon and Hendry were very receptive to this idea and therefore agreed when Eagle Star suggested sending senior staff to New Zealand to conduct an informal due diligence. "We were sure that the analysis would show that Sovereign was a good strong profitable company that was doing all the right things, and we were optimistic that Eagle Star would take a bigger stake in us," says Hendry. But after the Eagle Star team had reported back to head office, Lester got in touch with Coon and Hendry and instructed them to attend a meeting. "We were given 24 hours to be in Melbourne and told they were, in effect, going to take us over," says Hendry. "They said Sovereign had no real value and wasn't worth anything. They made us a ridiculously low offer and told us to take it or leave it." Eagle Star made it quite clear that if Hendry and Coon would not accept their offer, they would pull out of Sovereign completely leaving it without the funds, support and credibility it needed. "They really put a gun to our heads," says Coon. "They told us that they had been talking to people in Wellington and that if we didn't agree to their offer, we should be very worried. It was a very uncomfortable situation to be in."

But Eagle Star grossly underestimated their prey. Coon and Hendry had suspected for some time that the Australians would try to take control. They knew Lester's attitude towards minority investments, and they were also aware of the report from Eagle Star in England and its recommendation that it be taken over because of its potential. As part of their defence, they had enlisted David Belcher at Clavell Capital, to help them find another source of funding, and they had also approached Hannover Re, one of the world's largest re-insurance companies, about investing in Sovereign.

When they were summoned to Melbourne, Coon and Hendry took Belcher with them. Eagle Star was not impressed. They wanted nothing to do with Belcher and they refused to let him take part in the negotiations. "Belcher found the whole thing quite extraordinary," says Hendry. "He couldn't believe that people who were supposed to be your friends could actually behave in such a high-handed way." When Coon and Hendry insisted that Belcher sit in on the meetings or there would be no meetings at all, Eagle Star reluctantly agreed. In spite of Belcher's presence, Eagle Star were still confident the New Zealanders would be caught by surprise and, because they had no options, would have to accept their offer. In the meeting, Coon and Hendry were told they were losing their company, presented with the offer, and told "to sign here." To Eagle Star's amazement Coon and Hendry refused. They told an astounded Eagle Star that they had secured funds from Hannover Re and did not need Eagle Star's involvement in Sovereign. "Basically we told them to stick it," says Hendry with a roar of laughter. In reality, Hannover Re had not yet agreed to invest in Sovereign so Coon and Hendry left the door open for further negotiations with Eagle Star. "We had to be careful," says Coon. "We knew they were talking directly to the Government Actuary in Wellington and we knew that a few dirty tricks wasn't above their play. So we wanted to make it look as if we were still interested in doing a deal with them." In fact, Eagle Star had already threatened to tell the Government Actuary that Sovereign would not be able to continue in business if Eagle Star withdrew its support, which it was considering doing.

In December of 1990, Coon and Hendry finally ended the talks by telling Eagle Star that they had all the additional capital they needed from Hannover Re. Needless to say, Eagle Star was not happy. "They were absolutely furious," says Coon, his eyes twinkling. Eagle Star did not let go easily. They went as far as writing to Hannover Re and tried to scupper the arrangement but with no success. "Hannover Re was very relaxed and saw Eagle Star's interference for what it was," says Hendry. Even after they got nowhere with Hannover Re, Eagle Star continued to play hardball. They launched a number of legal actions against Sovereign, claiming that some of the actions management had taken were not consistent with the company's Articles of Association. "Their principle attack was on the basis that, by refusing their offer we, the managers, were acting in our best interests but not in the best interests of the company," explains Coon. Eagle Star also took a dim view of the fact all the negotiations with Hannover Re took place without the involvement or knowledge of their representative on the board and thus they had no information about the details of the agreement Coon and Hendry had entered into. "Fortunately we were able to defend ourselves against all allegations and ultimately they gave up," says Hendry. "We pointed out that because Eagle Star was acting in a predatory manner we were justified in excluding their representative from the negotiations." Eagle Star accepted this view and, realising these battles were getting them nowhere, took another tack. They decided that if they couldn't buy the company for a song, they would make Coon and Hendry pay a fortune to buy them out.

When Eagle Star presented their original ultimatum to Coon and Hendry, they told them Sovereign was worthless and therefore offered to pay only the par value ($1) for each of the 91.1% of the shares they did not own. Now that they wanted to be bought out, Eagle Star announced they believed the shares were worth $8 each. Not surprisingly, Coon and Hendry disagreed and made a counter offer of $2. The negotiations continued between Hendry and Reid for quite some period. Finally the board of Australian Eagle intervened. Perhaps because they felt he was not making any progress, the board became dissatisfied with John Reid as their representative on the Sovereign board, and in 1991, replaced him with Eagle Star's financial director, Neil Weeks. It was a difficult time for Weeks to come onto the board because the relationship between Eagle Star and Sovereign had deteriorated so badly. To his credit, Weeks adopted a more conciliatory 'let's forget the past and try to develop Sovereign' attitude which was warmly received by Coon and Hendry. "He was good value," says Hendry appreciatively. "We respected his interest and he was, I think, very instrumental in getting his CEO to think of Sovereign in more positive terms. We owe him something."

Although little progress was made in the negotiations between Eagle

Star and Sovereign during Weeks' time on the board, there was a marked improvement in the relationship between the two companies. Weeks indicated that Eagle Star recognised Sovereign's potential worth and therefore was interested in helping the company grow. But unfortunately Weeks was on the Sovereign board for only eight months and then he left Australian Eagle to take a more senior position with Eagle Star in England. Weeks was replaced by John Thomas whose attitude towards the negotiations with Sovereign was fortunately similar to Weeks'. He, too, saw that Sovereign was a company with a bright future and he let it be known that Eagle Star was now open to increasing its shareholding without needing to take over the company. But by then it was too late. Coon and Hendry had all the additional capital they needed from Hannover Re and they were not interested in reducing their equity any further. Because Coon and Hendry would not sell, and because it was still not possible to find a price acceptable to Eagle Star, the negotiations stalled. But because of the improvement in attitude towards Sovereign by Eagle Star and Thomas, Coon and Hendry were happy to let things continue to roll along.

Fortunes can change quickly in business.

Fortunes can change quickly in business. From the time Australian Eagle was trying to bully its way into winning control of Sovereign, through the period of the stalled negotiations, its parent company in England had been incurring losses in some of its worldwide operations. In 1992, Eagle Star decided to sell some of its assets to improve the company's financial performance and Australian Eagle was one of the first to be sold. The purchaser was QBE who, as a Fire & General insurance company, was not interested in the life division of Australian Eagle, and so once they had become the owners, QBE immediately sought a buyer for the life business, which of course included the 9.9% holding in Sovereign. Thomas let it be known to Coon and Hendry that his masters were keen to sell. Coon and Hendry went to Melbourne and taking advantage of their improved relationship with Eagle Star's senior managers, offered to purchase back the shares, at the price of $1 per share that Eagle Star had paid for them two years ago! To Coon and Hendry's surprise, their offer was accepted. "It was staggering," recalls Hendry still shaking his head with disbelief. "It was one of our finest hours."

With the buy back of Eagle Star's shares, a four-year chapter in Sovereign's history came to an end. In spite of winning a battle for their survival, Coon and Hendry were sad that the relationship with Eagle Star was over. "They were pretty important to us," Hendry acknowledges. "They certainly helped us get off the ground. If we hadn't been able to talk about Eagle Star being one of our shareholders and being supportive of us, it would have been much harder to get started. People were comforted initially by the fact that Eagle Star were there and we played on it pretty heavily." Ironically, the people at Eagle Star who tried to seize control of Sovereign had no jobs after Australian Eagle was sold, but Reid and Thomas survived.

The war with Eagle Star was over. The battle with the Securities Commission had been won. But another issue was demanding Coon and Hendry's attention.

This time the issue was within Sovereign itself.

CHAPTER 11

The revolution within

"It was a bold move, but anything we do at Sovereign is all or nothing. We have a life-time contract with our customers to give them the very best service we can."

By 1993, Coon and Hendry were aware that Sovereign had a major problem, and that problem was success. Apart from the on-going legal battles, Sovereign was on a roll. Eagle Star's takeover had been thwarted, the company kept developing successful new products and market share continued to grow. "Those days were brilliant," recalls David Whyte. "As soon as someone caught up with us and imitated our products, we just leapt forward." The Sovereign culture was now all about constant achievement. The drive was to outdo the last success, to be even more ambitious and to move very quickly from being a 'small niche operator' to becoming a significant market force. Coon and Hendry began to realise that as long as the attention of the Securities Commission did not hinder them, Sovereign could become a major player in the industry, perhaps even a predator gobbling up some of the traditional companies that had been slow to adapt to the new marketplace. The potential was huge and the future looked very exciting. But in the meantime, Sovereign lay in the no-man's land of being a mid-sized company. This did not sit easily with either Coon or Hendry because mid-sized companies could themselves become the targets for acquisition quite quickly. They feared they would lose control of both the strategic direction of the company and its day-to-day management if that were to happen. Ironically, the revolution that was about to take place within Sovereign would result in the very situation that Coon and Hendry wished to avoid, and yet would prove that their fears were groundless.

The aim was to move Sovereign from being a successful and dynamic life assurance company to being a major integrated financial services group, competing directly with not only their former foes, but with new ones such as banks and investment houses. Coon and Hendry knew that in the future, the competition would not just come from local players, who to a large extent had been easy targets, but from overseas based groups who were either setting up shop in New Zealand or buying existing New Zealand businesses. The problem for Hendry was to keep the Sovereign culture intact, particularly the key success factors such as service, intimacy, accountability and direct and open contact with key management, while at the same time allowing for more delegation, more responsibility and inevitably a more complex management and organisational structure. He knew that the transition from a flat management structure with a hands-on approach by those who knew, lived and breathed Sovereign, to a professionally managed, more complex organisation with a number of divisions that would compete for attention, resources, and control, would run the risk of turning Sovereign into the same type of beast with the unwieldy management structures and bureaucracies as the traditional life offices they had always criticised. Hendry understood that the new Sovereign had to be even more customer driven and efficient than the organisation it replaced. Most importantly, the transition between the old and the new organisation had to be seamless and done quickly.

The aim was to move Sovereign from being a successful and dynamic life assurance company to being a major integrated financial services group.

The drive to change was championed by both Hendry and Ballantyne, who was by then Sovereign's operations manager. In true Sovereign fashion, the revolution would be waged on two interrelated fronts: people and systems; and in two areas: administration and distribution. Ballantyne knew first hand the frustrations that administration functions produced if performed in the traditional way. When she joined Sovereign as a young and enthusiastic manager she purposefully set out to ensure Sovereign did not develop an operations structure that was overly bureaucratic. By the mid 1990, she had become political and ambitious, but she was also ruthlessly protective of Sovereign and very loyal to Coon and Hendry. She constantly strove for greater efficiencies and, like Coon and Hendry, believed these came from investing in people and technology. But she was even more passionate about looking after the customer than she was about increasing efficiency. "As the company grew it became more complex and it became more inefficient," says Ballantyne. "As a result, we were not always delivering what our customers needed. We knew we had to change."

Hendry had always believed that the key to a successful company was a managed blend of smart people working with even smarter information technology. This view had been behind Hendry's approach to managing Sovereign right from day one. But in the early years, everything was just in time. Key people were employed as they were needed and system development could barely keep up with the demand. Between dealing with the regulatory agencies, fighting off Eagle Star, building an adviser network and constantly reinventing the products, there was little time for scientific management. The needs of the minute meant that instinct and experience had to guide decisions. One exception was in dealing with the brokers who were, of course, Sovereign's key customers. Although Hendry was close to them and knew their needs and concerns, Sovereign conducted annual independent audits. These were qualitative type surveys, conducted face-to-face with randomly selected brokers by independent interviewers and were designed to be a combination of an information gathering and a problem-solving tool. While the results produced few surprises, the audits became an important tool in helping Sovereign to maintain its market edge through innovative products and 'knock your socks off' customer service.

In 1993, Hendry and Ballantyne decided to use the audit tool to test whether Sovereign's vision, strategic direction and business objectives were understood by key staff within the company, particularly by those who would be an essential to changing the way the company was managed. A questionnaire was developed by Sovereign's marketing consultants and posted to 26 staff at all levels throughout the company. The reaction to the audit was extremely positive with staff finding the experience of being consulted refreshing. Many of the comments that came back were more frank than had been expected. Broadly speaking, the questionnaire was developed to serve as a benchmark to test each person's understanding of the company's direction, mission and purpose, because if greater empowerment of staff was to be the goal, it was essential that everyone was headed in the same direction according to a shared vision. The survey also examined how well each person felt they fitted into a team, and whether they, along with their team-mates, felt they could contribute to the achievement of Sovereign's business goals. This was a very important aspect of the audit because Ballantyne's notion of a 'smarter' organisation involved a true team function where people understood not only their role in their team, but also the bigger picture of the role the team played in meeting

Sovereign's growth objectives. Ballantyne took the idea of the 'little person making the big difference' very seriously. This was not a fad she paid lip-service to, but rather a goal she constantly spoke about, worried about and sought to make happen. Ballantyne also knew that businesses succeeded because they operated effective processes and that, since processes were operated by teams rather than by individuals, it was critical that each person understood the team's process and their part in making it work. This, she realised, would be even more important as the business became increasingly complex, and the industry was faced with growing regulatory and compliance requirements.

On a more personal level, the survey looked at what each person's career aspirations and feelings of fulfilment might be. Sovereign wanted people to be ambitious, and they wanted to employ people who had a sense of hunger. They also wanted people to have a realistic understanding of where their talents lay and where they might constructively and successfully put their skills to work. Ironically, a by-product of raising this issue was that people who did not have what Hendry and Ballantyne considered to be the right stuff began to leave the company. On the other hand, those who did have the talents Sovereign needed were encouraged to participate more and their contribution was rewarded. Participants in the survey were also asked what they perceived to be their opportunities for growth and advancement, and how they wished to have their efforts and achievements recognised. Sovereign had been generous in how performance was rewarded from its inception, particularly in terms of remuneration. These areas were important to Hendry and Ballantyne because right from the beginning they aimed to create a culture that balanced encouraging people to be ambitious, with helping them to understand their own limits, and which also rewarded performance generously.

There were some fundamental problems that needed to be fixed if Hendry and Ballantyne were to be successful in re-shaping Sovereign.

The results from the internal audit were mixed. On the positive side, the survey revealed there was a good level of understanding of the company's mission statement. More importantly, it showed that staff had bought into Coon and Hendry's vision. "The survey showed there was a high level of commitment to the company's direction and a buying into what Sovereign stood for and sought to achieve,"

Whitney recalls. On the other hand, the survey indicated there were some fundamental problems that needed to be fixed if Hendry and Ballantyne were to be successful in re-shaping Sovereign. One clearly identified problem was that staff throughout the company felt there was a need for much greater communication. Neither Coon nor Hendry were particularly good communicators, Coon because he preferred to work with numbers and Hendry because he was too interested in doing things to take the time to talk about them. As one staff member said in the survey, "Hendry won't delegate and can't teach." Some of the lapses in communication were justifiable of course because in the early days there was little need to keep people informed. The office was so small everyone could hear what was going on or simply walk into Hendry's office and talk to him if they had a question. To his credit, Hendry saw this as a weakness and made a concerted effort to improve his communication style. More importantly, the company instituted a process for internal communication that included, among other things, monthly meetings for all staff held late Friday afternoons followed by drinks. These were usually led by Ballantyne or Hendry.

The audit had brought Sovereign's symptoms clearly into the open, and the findings confirmed what Hendry and Ballantyne had known intuitively. They also knew the cure would involve taking a radically different approach to Sovereign's business and would require a dramatic re-structuring of staff around work processes, and the re-engineering of those processes. The revolution had begun.

Leaving Ballantyne to lead the internal changes, Hendry and Coon turned their attention to two new initiatives they were launching in the marketplace, which, if successful, would transform Sovereign.

CHAPTER 12
The best laid schemes

*"The best laid schemes o' mice an' men.
Gang aft a-gley."*
Robert Burns

Life assurance is a very capital-intensive business. Coon and Hendry had been able to launch Sovereign with very little capital thanks to the arrangements Coon had made with some of the world's leading reassurance companies. Companies such as Gerling Globale, Cologne Re and Hannover Re had agreed to pay Sovereign commissions on every new policy sold which allowed Sovereign to meet its cash flow and capital requirements in the early days. Coon and Hendry knew that there would be a need for additional capital to fund future growth. By 1994, Sovereign had reached that point.

Coon and Hendry believed that the best solution to the problem of how to raise more capital was for Sovereign to list on the New Zealand Stock Exchange (NZSE) and become a public company. This would allow them to raise more capital through selling shares, and also to retain control of the company because they would have the largest shareholding. "We had several funding options in place but we viewed a public listing as the most advantageous," says Coon. Consequently, they decided to make an initial public offering (IPO) on the NZSE, with the listing date to be November 1994. "At the time of our decision to go down the listing path, the stock market was buoyant and all economic indicators and advice pointed to us achieving a successful public float," says Coon. The broking firm CS First Boston, which was appointed to manage the listing process, was very optimistic about Sovereign's listing prospects.

What Coon and Hendry did not realise was how tortuous the path to a public listing would be, what a toll it would take both on them personally and on the business, and how little would result from their efforts. A stock market listing is a brutal process. It involves baring the corporate soul through the process of due diligence, and it demands an extraordinary amount of time and resources from key people throughout the organisation to keep the listing process on track for the listing date. In Sovereign's case the burden for managing the listing process fell with Coon and Hendry, of course, and also Coon's brother, Richard.

Richard Coon came to New Zealand with his family in 1994. He had been an early investor in Sovereign and he wanted to help with the public listing. He was offered a six-month contract, which grew into 12 months, and was later offered a permanent position as finance director. An MBA graduate from Harvard Business School with a background in corporate finance and merchant banking, he had worked for both small and large companies overseas. One of the aspects about Sovereign that appealed to him was its culture. "I am basically an entrepreneurial sort of person," he says, "and I liked the friendly, family, democratic atmosphere of the company. It was a can-do company with the smell of success in the air," he adds. One of Richard Coon's main strengths is that he is skilled in analysing financial risks and opportunities. "Richard has played a major role in Sovereign's success," says Hendry. "He excels in managing high level financial strategies and he is able to work on several major projects simultaneously." Richard Coon was involved in setting up the financial systems that allowed for the group's later expansion, and he was very involved in the 1994 listing. In fact, from the time he joined Sovereign in 1994, he has been centrally involved in every major strategic initiative and financial transaction that has taken place.

The experience of listing on the NZSE was not a happy one for Sovereign.

The experience of listing on the NZSE was not a happy one for Sovereign. For a start, the lead brokers who have a set way of doing things control the process, and often there is a clash of cultures between the company listing and the brokers, lawyers and accountants involved in the listing process. The Sovereign experience was no different. "There was arrogance and disregard from the outsiders managing the listing process," says Whitney. "Everything was done very much the way they've always done it. There was no consideration given to the Sovereign way of doing business." At a crucial time in Sovereign's listing process, when Coon and Hendry were overseas promoting the share float among potential offshore investors, the brokers saw an opportunity to seize control of the marketing of the listing. "These were the darkest days of the listing process," Whitney recalls. "Although it had been agreed that Sovereign's own marketing people would have an involvement, CS First Boston rode roughshod over them." On hearing about the disregard CS First Boston was showing to the Sovereign people, Chairman Dennis Ferrier moved in. "One of his finest, and final, acts for Sovereign," says Whitney, "was to summon the key outside people into the board room and read the riot act. He then fired the external marketing people, and appointed his own contacts from the public relations company Network Communications to take over the media liaison and media management process." Sadly, not long after this Ferrier passed away.

The other problem was that the timing was not right. Shortly after Coon and Hendry had decided to list, the Asian economies went into a severe recession. The investment community around the world retrenched and there was very little interest in the Sovereign float. "Against all expectations, at the critical time we needed to make the final decision to go ahead with the public listing," says Coon, "the New Zealand stock market was suffering a downturn. To make matters worse, a large number of other companies were seeking listing at the same time," he adds. As a result, Coon and Hendry believed they had no option but to cancel the listing. "There had been an enormous commitment of human and financial resources to getting ready to list," says Hendry. "Pulling the plug was a major financial and psychological blow." But the aborted listing was not the only setback for Coon and Hendry that year. Indeed, 1994 was to turn out to be a year of disappointment for the company.

At some stage, most successful New Zealand companies turn their eyes towards Australia. If it worked in New Zealand, the thinking goes, then it will probably work in Australia. And since the market is much bigger, the potential rewards are likely to be much greater too. In 1994, Coon and Hendry decided to cross the Tasman and enter the Australian market. "Strategically we saw moving to a new market as beneficial for securing Sovereign's future, both locally and internationally," says Coon, "and we could see a window of opportunity to establish a Sovereign operation in Australia."

Based on market research that had been done for them, Coon and Hendry's aim was to replicate in Australia everything that they had done in New Zealand, but with the administration to be done in New Zealand. "We believed that the products we had developed in New

Zealand would be just as popular in Australia," says Hendry, "and that the service we provided brokers would be as well received as it had been in New Zealand. By doing the administration in New Zealand," he adds, "we believed we could achieve economies of scale that would further enhance the profitability of Sovereign."

Sovereign Australia's offices were located in Epping, New South Wales, and a strong management team was recruited under the leadership of Andrew Wakeling. Wakeling was formerly with the AMP and had been a colleague of Coon's at Bacon & Woodrow in England. John Thomas, who had been with Australian Eagle during the days when they owned part of Sovereign and who had been on the Sovereign board, was appointed sales and marketing director. Early signs were promising. Sovereign Australia attracted enthusiastic support from nationwide networks of advisers. "As a result, we had a high level of confidence in our ability to attract new business," says Hendry. Planning moved into high gear and the intention was to open for business in early 1995.

The aim was to replicate in Australia everything that they had done in New Zealand.

As with the New Zealand public listing, events were to force Coon and Hendry to abandon ship. "Again, the unexpected frustrated our plans," says Coon. The problem was that Sovereign Australia's strategy was to target the individual personal superannuation market, "but the government introduced compulsory superannuation and that market was wiped out overnight," says Hendry with disgust. With the demise of personal superannuation schemes, the competition for risk business became intense. Much as is happening in New Zealand today, companies lowered their rates and increased their commissions in a desperate attempt to attract business. "Our assessment was that it would be impossible to trade profitably in that market environment," says Hendry. In December 1994, just weeks after abandoning the share float, Coon and Hendry decided to withdraw from Australia. With the money that had been invested in setting up shop in Australia, and with the generous severance packages that were paid out to staff, this became another very costly and time-consuming exercise.

Coon and Hendry were personally very disappointed, both in the failed Australian venture and the aborted public listing. "At the start of the year, our sights were firmly set on two major projects – seeking a public listing and launching an Australian operation," says Hendry. "We strongly believed these initiatives would increase Sovereign's standing in the marketplace by increasing our profile and widening the base of our operations. It was a major disappointment to us that neither came to fruition." It had also been a major distraction for them both, and a significant cause of stress. As with the battles with the Securities Commission, Coon and Hendry bore the burden of developing these initiatives themselves, so that Sovereign staff were able to focus on the business of servicing advisers and policyholders. As a result, in spite of everything that had happened, Sovereign produced another set of outstanding sales and financial results in 1994.

That is not to say that it was business as usual inside Sovereign. It was a period of constant and rapid change. Ballantyne was making sure of that.

CHAPTER 13

Meanwhile, Sovereign re-invents itself

"Sovereign's success will come from having a business strategy and human resource strategy working in total harmony and coordination."

While Coon and Hendry were trying to launch Sovereign Australia and at the same time take Sovereign public in New Zealand, Ballantyne was reinventing Sovereign internally. This revolution in administration was built around a Total Quality Management (TQM) philosophy. Hendry knew that in the service industry you were only as good as your last success and that regardless of the unprecedented growth in business, the service commitments and expectations of brokers and their clients would continue to rise. Get this wrong and any loyalty that had been accrued would soon disappear. He therefore believed that quality would be the key point of differentiation between Sovereign and its competitors.

This view was confirmed by an informal review conducted at Hendry's request by David Anderson. Anderson had worked in the life assurance industry in the U.K. since 1973. Like so many expatriates who ended up at Sovereign, his wife was a New Zealander. By the mid 1990s, the Andersons had decided they would like to move back to New Zealand and David began the process of looking for a job. A friend suggested he contact Coon and they met on one of Anderson's trips to New Zealand. Hendry joined the meeting, which lasted only 15 or 20 minutes. Hendry told him they had no openings for him and Anderson returned to Britain to consider one or two other job offers. Ten days later, Hendry rang with the offer of a job and they met in London to discuss it further. "There was no title for my position and no job description either," says Anderson. " But I had liked Chris and been impressed with Ian. I also recognised the potential for Sovereign to become a major financial services company."

Anderson joined Sovereign in September of 1994 with the title of corporate planning manager and was charged with the task of producing a report outlining Sovereign's strengths and weaknesses. "For five or six weeks I wandered about the place with an exercise book, talking to people, attending meetings and observing," Anderson recalls. It was not an easy assignment as some people saw him as a threat but he learned a great deal which he reported back to Hendry in his weekly meetings with him. "The first thing I noticed," says Anderson, "was a lack of processes. There was plenty of creativity, flair, youth and technology, but no processes. Everyone seemed to do their own thing." Anderson observed that meetings were run without an agenda and that Hendry seemed to have made his mind up even before the meetings began. He also saw that emphasis was placed on developing managers' knowledge but there was little attention paid to developing their skills. Overall, Anderson concluded that Sovereign was in serious need of a shake-up.

Both Hendry and Ballantyne saw TQM as the key to addressing the issues Ballantyne's audit and Anderson's walkabout had identified. In one sense this was not new, since from the beginning Sovereign had based its operations on quality and service as the criteria by which the company's business performance would be judged. But now quality became a formal policy. Unlike many companies, quality at Sovereign was not merely the flavour of the month to which lip service was paid. Hendry and Ballantyne were determined to create an environment where creativity and quality would flourish, and where individuals would accept responsibility for delivering outstanding client service. They would achieve this by creating a new management structure and by implementing TQM tools such as teamwork, process monitoring and continuous improvement.

A formalised strategic plan for re-structuring Sovereign was developed by a corporate services group led by Hendry and Ballantyne. Its implementation became the responsibility of Ballantyne and South African-import Chris Breytenbach. With a doctorate from South Africa, he had both the academic horsepower and practical experience to help the less formally trained Ballantyne bring about the revolution. The Breytenbachs became a family act at Sovereign with sons Pieter and Johannes both joining the company as well. Each one had experience with strategic planning and change management practices. The Breytenbachs later created a stand-alone consulting facility within Sovereign called Sovereign Solutions, which would later become part of the change management function throughout the group. This was perhaps the first evidence of the 'intrapreneurship' within the

Sovereign group that Hendry was trying to develop.

Breytenbach was soon talking up the process of change with gusto. His approach to implementation was guided by the belief that Sovereign's success would come from (1) having a coordinated business strategy and human resource strategy, and (2) empowering individuals within Sovereign to take responsibility for their actions and their role in the company's future.

"This process makes Sovereign the best company I have ever worked with. It convinces me that nothing will stop Sovereign's future progress."

"Sovereign's success," he said, "will come from having a business strategy and human resource strategy working in total harmony and coordination." He realized that empowering individuals to take responsibility for their actions and for their role in the company's future, was a bold initiative, and he was extremely positive about the outcome. "We have ensured that the process has remained pragmatic, simple, but very effective," he said, "and this process makes Sovereign the best company I have ever worked with. It convinces me that nothing will stop Sovereign's future progress."

Ballantyne and Breytenbach understood that the driver for the restructuring was the need to take Sovereign from being a niche player to being a major company in the financial services market. This would mean rapid growth and, therefore, their primary aim was to create within Sovereign a process where senior management managed further expansion proactively rather than reacted to market forces. This was where TQM played a pivotal role and one of the guiding principles of TQM, do the right thing right each and every time, became part of the Sovereign culture. This principle was linked back to Sovereign's vision to be "a provider of quality financial services whose values earn the respect and trust of its clients by being profitable, efficient and a friend for life," and to its mission "to nurture an environment within which creativity and quality flourishes and individuals accept personal responsibility for delivering outstanding client service."

Ballantyne and Breytenbach articulated a number of key principles by which Sovereign would be run:

- Provide customer service of the highest quality;
- Build long-term relationships with professional financial intermediaries;
- Provide quality leadership and effective team action;
- Have strong commitment to the development of skilled, motivated people;
- Show honesty, integrity and creativity in our activities;
- Demonstrate commitment to efficiency, productivity and quality;
- Make a commitment to continuous improvement;
- Be at the forefront of harnessing technology.

To make sure these actually happened, they defined a number of key indicators, which would be monitored by management. These included personal growth, teamwork (involving such values as caring, cooperation and participation), individual responsibility, pride (being the best and loving it), and recognition and excellence (doing better today than yesterday).

Ballantyne led by example. She made sure that the operations area, which was her primary responsibility, was at the forefront of restructuring the organisation, implementing TQM practices, and fostering innovation. As she looked hard at her own area, Ballantyne began to see that operations was still departmentalised and not sufficiently customer focused. Having people in departments such as underwriting, new business, policy issuing and broker liaison work in teams helped lift performance but the department was still inefficient. "We were still struggling with a traditional functional structure," she recalls. "Whenever we hired another person, we got only half a person in increased productivity. The problem was the structure." Of even greater concern to Ballantyne, who is absolutely passionate about customer service, was that the traditional functional structure still allowed activities to fall between the cracks as work was handed off from one team to another. Worse still, when there was a problem, brokers were still shunted from pillar to post as each team denied responsibility for the problem. "I took a telephone call from a broker one day who was wanting to check up on something," she says cringing at the memory of it. "He couldn't find anyone who would take responsibility for his problem. I asked around and I couldn't either! No one knew anything. I was so frustrated. Then I thought, if I feel like that in my own department, how must our brokers feel? We had to change."

Ballantyne's solution, which she implemented in 1995, was to create a TEAM structure (standing for Total Excellence in Administration and Management). This involved setting up multi-disciplined teams, called business units, which would each look after a pool of brokers. "I had been reading about self-managed teams," says Ballantyne, "and I could see the benefits to our customers if our teams were multi-skilled. I wanted people to be accountable and to take responsibility. I thought the ideal structure would be one staff member dedicated to a group of brokers. Because of the wide range of skills involved this wasn't possible so the result was the business units."

> *"I wanted people to be accountable and to take responsibility."*

According to a written project plan submitted by Ballantyne to Sovereign's board, the objectives of the TEAM project were to:

1. Change the current structure to inter-dependent self managed business units;
2. Provide staff with a defined and definite career development path based on competence;
3. Redesign the reward structure;
4. Set in place a coaching and mentoring support function for the business units;
5. Design and implement a competency-based training certification system.

A team of six people, including Ballantyne, led the project and Breytenbach managed its implementation. Ballantyne was responsible for developing the career development path, Errol Timmins, a long-standing employee developed the coaching and mentoring support, Johannes Breytenbach, Chris Breytenbach's son, designed the competency-based training system, Michelle Milham led the change to self-managed business units and Ted Gruebner provided logistical support. In typical Ballantyne fashion, the performance targets were challenging. The processing of new policy applications and policy alterations was to be reduced from the current 48 hour turnaround currently achieved 80% of the time to a 24 hour turnaround to be achieved 90% of the time. Answering customer queries and providing quotations was to improve from a 24hr turnaround 80% of the time to instant answers delivered 90% of the time.

The business units consisted of seven to eight person teams representing the functional areas of New Business, Policy Servicing, Broker/Adviser Liaison and Underwriting. The term business unit was used to convey to staff that they were now no longer just responsible for performing an administrative task, they were responsible for working together with their team mates to operate a small business within the overall Sovereign business. Each business unit had a team leader who coordinated the work. "I had thought of going to self-managed teams," says Ballantyne, "but then I decided I didn't want to go that far. I wanted each team to have a leader who was there to develop their people, to act as a mentor. I also wanted someone available for customers who wanted to deal with a 'manager'." Five such business units were created and each was given responsibility for looking after the needs of a specific group of advisers and their clients. "All clerks became customer service consultants," Ballantyne recalls. "This made a big difference to the policyholders who got the feeling they were talking to someone important who was focused on their problems." Leading edge technology was developed to allow each business unit to look after the requirements of over 1,000 advisors and a growing client base.

The development of business units was very successful. Policy processing was done with increased efficiency but more importantly, service to advisers improved dramatically. Each adviser was given a telephone number that would take them directly to the team who handled their business. When they called, any inquiry or problem they had was handled by the team who became a one-stop-shop whether the problem was having a policy application approved by underwriting, the actual policy being sent to the customer, or the broker receiving their commission cheque. Within each team, members started to become multi-skilled so that the team could continue to function effectively even if one of its members was absent. Job satisfaction increased because staff were looking after people not processing paper, and also because they began to develop relationships with the brokers they served. "Staff also got a buzz from having a role clearly focused on the customers," says Ballantyne. "They really enjoyed the broker contact. We even sent a photo of the team to the brokers they were looking after." When service delivery problems did occur, the team would meet with a number of brokers and sought out the problem. For the brokers, doing business with Sovereign meant dealing with a small team of people they knew, rather than with a faceless company full of strangers. Sovereign had found a way to handle a large amount of business in exactly the way it had done when it was a small company. As business increased, all that had to be done was to create new business units.

> *Within each team, members started to become multi-skilled so that the team could continue to function effectively even if one of its members was absent.*

At the same time as she was reorganising the operations area, Ballantyne questioned the way the work itself was being done. She saw inefficiencies due to files being bottle necked in one area and therefore not allowing work to be done on some other aspect of the policy. Time was wasted looking for files that could be on any one of a number of desks if they were not in the filing cabinet. Often wads of paper had to be waded through to find the information someone was seeking and sometimes the file became disorganised in the process. Worse, bits of paper became separated from the main file and were occasionally lost. In 1993, Ballantyne suggested creating a paperless office through an IT process called imaging. "It was a bold move," says Ballantyne. "But anything we do at Sovereign is all or nothing. We have a life-time contract with our customers to give them the very best service we can." A project team involving staff in both Operations, Marketing and IT was put in place to develop the software and administrative processes to convert all paper into an electronic image that could be handled in a windows environment on a network of computers. Once the system was implemented, files could be worked on simultaneously by a number of people, and for each of them information was just a keystroke away. Everyone on the network could then see the updated information and there was no chance of losing vital bits of paper. Another benefit was that the time taken to process files could be easily monitored. This allowed managers to monitor key performance indicators related to processing efficiency, and also to regulate workflows. If they saw that one business unit was temporarily snowed under, they would re-direct some of the routine work to another team, which was not quite so busy at that moment. This again improved customer service by minimising delays.

One of the major challenges facing Sovereign staff in implementing the 'paperless office' was getting the outside IT contractors to understand what they needed them to do. It took six months to develop the system, which was then tried out in one business unit for three months until the bugs were ironed out. The second challenge was getting people to use it. "They were apprehensive at first," says Ballantyne. "People weren't sure they could spend all day looking at a computer screen. But once they started using it, they quickly saw the benefits." Lyn Dorreen agrees. "I was all for it," she says. "We noticed we weren't servicing the brokers properly and we saw the advantages for both brokers and ourselves alike." Looking back, Ballantyne believes the key to the successful introduction of the new technology was to phase it in and to involve people in its implementation.

Becoming a paperless office was a huge task but it was an option that Sovereign had that none of its competitors did. Because it was a young company, Sovereign did not have decades of files in its archives and that meant that retrospective scanning of old files, although a chore, was possible. The traditional life companies, which had been around for over a hundred years in some cases, could not even contemplate such a task. Thus the only option for them was to pick some point in time and scan documents from that time forward. This would have the effect of creating two systems, which would bring with it a new set of problems, risks and inefficiencies. In fact, it was so important to Sovereign that they have only one system that when they bought out MetLife, they retrospectively scanned over 60,000 files.

Ballantyne also turned her attention to activities outside Sovereign that were impacting on operational efficiency. One of these was the process by which prospective purchasers of life insurance provided medical information. This is a problem for companies around the world because it creates a log jam in the application-acceptance process. Medical examinations, once the sole domain of doctors, meant that life companies were at the mercy of doctors, who despite being well-paid for their efforts, would treat filling out a complicated medical form as their lowest priority. Ballantyne became familiar with a system being used by a company in Australia that fast tracked this process thereby improving service to both prospective policy-holders who wanted the policy issued quickly, and brokers who wanted their commission cheques yesterday. Based on this model Ballantyne developed Healthscreen, which took the clearance process out of the hands of doctors and put it into the company through the use of a mobile team of nurses. These nurses visit clients on their home ground and conduct the medical examination themselves, even to the point of taking blood and urine samples. This is often done under challenging circumstances. One nurse had to meet a truck driver in the middle of the road. His measurements were taken by putting the scales on the road beside his cab and he went off into the bushes to produce the urine sample. Another went to see a Canterbury farmer on a cold wet winter's day and found him working in one of his back paddocks. "I came back with mud up to my knees," she says. "After that, I always carried a pair of gumboots with me and I have worn them lots of times since!" If there are no complications, Healthscreen makes the procedure for issuing a policy much faster, thereby saving Sovereign a considerable sum of money in the process. It is a classic win-win situation for both the company and the customers, although one customer was not so sure. The 70-year-old man said he would not use Healthscreen. "I don't want my premium loaded because my blood pressure was elevated because it was taken by some pretty young nurse!" he explained. The nurses, themselves, are passionate about the role they play in being the company's caring face since they know they are making the policy application procedure quicker and easier for their customers. Healthscreen also provides the company with more accurate information since clients are more comfortable and open with the nurses than with a sales person. "Also, it is harder to lie to a nurse than a form," say the nurses laughing.

Sovereign was the first life company in New Zealand to introduce a service like Healthscreen, and once again it revolutionised the industry by challenging the conventional ways of doing things. Initially, Healthscreen was available in only the major centres but today it operates throughout the country. Nurses have more recently become even more involved in looking after Sovereign's customers. They frequently deliver claims cheques to claimants, thus putting a human face to the claims process as well. The development of Healthscreen is a good example of the Sovereign approach to business: identify a problem, look for the best most innovative system in the world, and adapt it to the New Zealand conditions.

Another opportunity that Ballantyne saw to steal the march on its competition was the way agents were paid their commissions. Normal industry practice was for brokers to be paid weekly but this caused a bottleneck in administration. "Under that system, the work load was not very evenly spread," says Ian Perry, team leader for one of the business units. "Proposals would come in on Mondays and Tuesdays

Sovereign House in Takapuna on Auckland's North Shore. This has been the home of Sovereign Assurance since 1990.

REALITY IS CRAZY

Ian Hendry and Chris Coon on the balcony of their new office in Sovereign House in 1990.

Naomi Ballantyne

Don Jefferies

David Whyte

Ross Wallace

Russell Hutchinson

Stephen Potter

John Lamb

Errol Timmins

Michelle Milham

Lyn Dorreen

Ted Gruebner

Some of Sovereign's first staff members, 1989 – 1990.

Sovereign's board of directors in 1992. From left to right, Chris Coon, Dennis Ferrier and Ian Hendry.

Erich Bachmann, taken in 1989.

Bruce Bornholdt, taken in 1995.

Management team-building in 1991 at Puka Park Lodge. From left to right, Ian Hendry, Chris Coon, Naomi Ballantyne and David Whyte.

Advisers and their partners who were members of Sovereign Assurance's first overseas expedition, destined for Hong Kong in March 1990.

Sovereign has always been an enthusiastic supporter of Dragon Boat racing. Pictured is one of the company's earlier teams. Today, members of the Dragon Boat team are paid up to $30,000 per year to travel around New Zealand to compete in events.

REALITY IS CRAZY
110

Some of Sovereign's key people in 1996-1997.

Above, the operations managers. From left to right: Naidu Lalitha, Ted Gruebner, Deanna Defina, Errol Timmins, Jo Hutchinson, Grant Willis, Michelle Milham, Naomi Ballantyne, Kaye Smith, Elaine Farnham and Gary Bishop.

Left: MetLife managers.
From left to right: Ernie Uganecz, Peter Fitzsimmons and Roger Adams.

Below: Managers in sales, distribution and broker development. From left to right: Peter Harrison, Alan Harrington, Steve Shrigley, Barry Rose, Chris Carnall, Michelle Doyle, Mike Barnes, David Haak, Antony Marsh, Tim Arrowsmith, David Anderson, Peter Letica and Mike Gudsell.

Taken at Sovereign's black tie Christmas function, 1998. Seated from left to right: Catherine and David Belcher, Jeanette Bornholdt, Ian and June Hendry; standing, Mike and Jo Walsh, Bruce Bornholdt, Jane and Richard Coon.

Taken at Sovereign's black tie Christmas function, 1999. Seated from left to right: Jenny Uganecz, Jo and Mike Walsh, Pam Norris; standing, Ernie Uganecz, Chris Coon, June Hendry, Ralph Norris, Yvonne Coon and Ian Hendry.

REALITY IS CRAZY

112

Sovereign sponsors over 30 staff sports teams. Pictured here are teams from Dragon Boating, tennis, netball, rugby and the hockey team, shown forming a pyramid.

REALITY IS CRAZY

113

REALITY IS CRAZY

114

The Hart and Soul roadshow, an informative and motivational event featuring former All Black coach, John Hart, held for independent advisers in 1999.

Independent advisers enjoying Sovereign's hospitality at the FPIA conference in Christchurch, 2001.

Sovereign has always believed that investing in its people is one of the best ways to grow the business. Here are some team building moments.

REALITY IS CRAZY

116

Every year Sovereign holds a mid-year extravaganza for staff. These scenes are from the 2000 event based on the television programme, 'Stars in your eyes'.

REALITY IS CRAZY

117

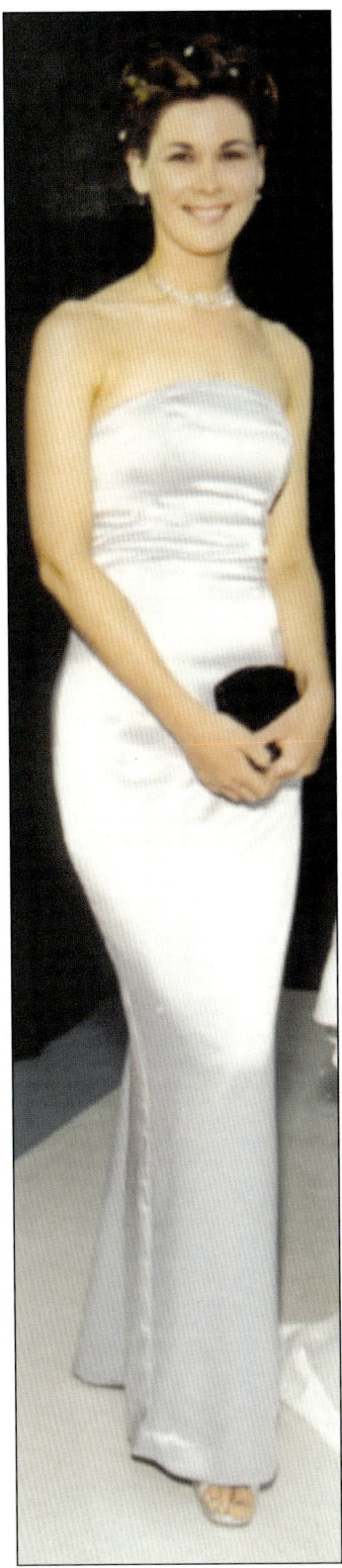

Sovereign hosts a black tie Christmas party each year. These scenes are from the 2000 event in Auckland. For the first time, that year there was also a Wellington event due to the merger with Colonial.

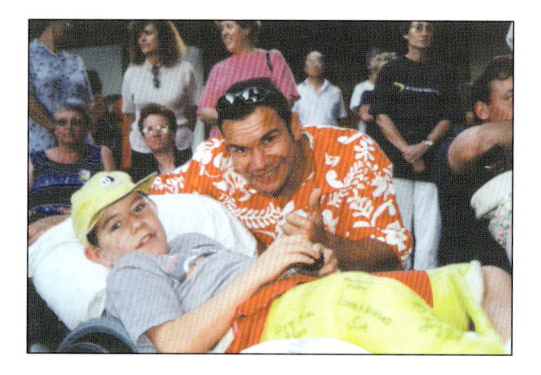

Here are some of the organisations to have benefited from Sovereign sponsorship. Above, the Heart Foundation and the Wilson Home. Below, the Ellerslie Flower Show. Opposite page, top, Sovereign Cornwall Cricket Club; middle, the Auckland Blues; below, the Whangamata Surf Life Saving Club.

REALITY IS CRAZY

REALITY IS CRAZY

120

Each year Sovereign puts on a children's Christmas party for staff.
Like all Sovereign functions, it is a gala event.

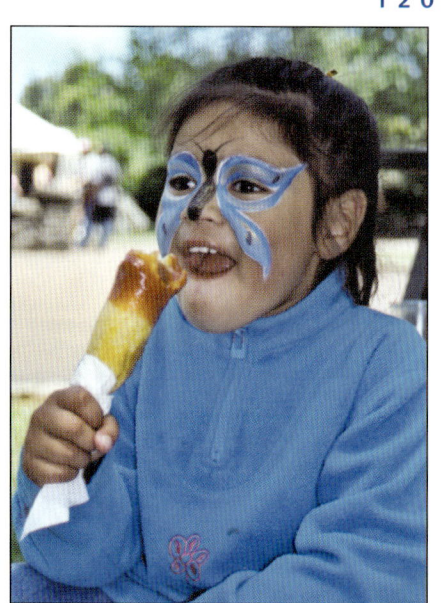

but pay day was Wednesdays". Ballantyne developed a system for paying brokers their commissions on a daily basis, which had the effect of smoothing out the workflow.

Hendry had always believed that smart people working with smart systems would lead to business success. Accordingly, over the years Sovereign has devoted a large amount of money and a great deal of effort to developing world class IT systems, which have made it easy for both brokers and policyholders to obtain information about their policies, commissions and claims. They have also made it possible for advisers in the field to transact business with Sovereign remotely and in real time. The paperless office that Sovereign created coupled with interactive systems means that through a telephone connection the Sovereign files and systems are literally only a keyboard stroke away, even if the adviser and his customer are in Balclutha.

In 1995, after several years of development, Sovereign launched the first of its external IT initiatives under the banner of Window On Our World software. The initial package was a comprehensive quotation programme designed to provide advisers in the field with the ability to manage and process client proposals themselves. Like the Underwriter's Guide, this move helped to demystify the underwriting process and take much of the decision-making away from head office, putting it directly into the hands of advisers. Over the years, the depth and sophistication of these programmes have continued to evolve. First, Sovereign Remote Communications (SRC), which supplied policy data direct to an adviser's PC, offered an up-to-the minute policy, proposal and diary inquiry facility. This linked the adviser directly to a Sovereign business unit support person, and offered general on-line help. SRC evolved into a more complex initiative branded PlatformZ. This management software tool, designed and developed by Sovereign for its advisers, incorporated a client database, time management systems, reporting systems and the means to manage their own marketing campaigns.

Once again Sovereign revolutionised the life industry by challenging the conventional ways of doing things.

From this early work, Sovereign would become a world leader in software development in the life assurance industry. It was a case of necessity mothering invention. "The problem was that any software we bought from anyone else never worked," says Hendry. "So, we had a corporate philosophy of developing our own and this has always worked very well for us."

Each of Sovereign's systems has been developed with one clear aim, and that is to improve the level of service Sovereign provides to its advisers, which, in turn, will make their dealings with policyholders more efficient, more productive and more positive. The main problem Sovereign has encountered throughout this technology development is the cost. It costs as much money to develop an IT system for one user as for one million, and Sovereign has found itself having to commit large sums of money for systems that would be used by relatively small numbers of people. That Sovereign has been able to accomplish what it has in information technology systems is astounding when you consider that the driving force behind the mergers of many insurance companies world-wide is the IT costs.

At the same time that Ballantyne and Breytenbach were revolutionising Sovereign's administrative processes, David Anderson was tackling the sales and distribution side of the business. After his brief stint as corporate planning manager, Anderson was made general manager of broker development. Anderson had not been looking for a job in sales, but by 1995 it became clear that Sovereign had some performance problems in this area. Like most life companies, Sovereign had a broker development manager in each of the major centres of New Zealand. These were salaried employees and their role was to influence independent brokers to place their business with Sovereign, just as Hendry and Whyte had done when Sovereign first opened for business. "After Whyte left Sovereign, the growth in sales slowed, and I believed a large part of the problem was the way the broker development managers were paid," says Anderson. "So, I formed a committee of development managers to agree on the principles for a new pay system. This got their buy-in and the committee identified twelve issues that needed to be addressed to make the new system work." Anderson made the necessary changes and the new system quickly led to increased sales.

"I believed a large part of the problem was the way the broker development managers were paid."

Anderson's second priority when he took on the job of general manager broker development was to increase the development managers' skills. "The way we used to influence brokers was very primitive," he recalls. "It was simply one of going around all the broker companies and wining and dining the brokers." Anderson's approach was to teach the development managers how to help the brokers to grow their own businesses. Anderson understood that brokers were not interested in selling Sovereign products, rather they were interested in building successful businesses for themselves. If Sovereign could help brokers to do that, he reasoned, then the brokers would form a relationship with Sovereign and recommend Sovereign's products to their clients. "I told the development managers that their task was not to persuade the brokers to shift their business to Sovereign but to help the brokers grow their business," says Anderson. Anderson and his team also developed some generic business products and services, for example strategic planning tools that the development managers took out to the brokers. The first development manager to embrace this approach was David Haak who replaced Anderson when he left the company for health reasons in 1999. Haak coached 20 brokers in strategic planning, and when they saw how well the brokers reacted, the other development managers readily started using these tools. Before long, managers were working with as many as 170 brokers, helping them to be more successful business people. Sovereign eventually produced a manual that development managers could use to teach brokers how to run more effective businesses by developing business and marketing plans, and by implementing administrative systems and processes. "This manual was a world first," says Anderson with pride. "It was really exciting because it showed the broker development managers that there was a different way of doing their jobs."

Sovereign's internal revolution brought about the improvements both in the administrative and sales areas that Hendry had been looking for. The re-structuring of management, the TEAM philosophy, the creation of the business units, and the move to a paperless office had all contributed to improvement in service performance even though larger volumes of business were being handled. In a series of independent industry surveys conducted by Australian-based WA Taylor and Associates, Sovereign scored at the top in all service criteria. Staff felt empowered, and as a result of multi-skilling, much more a part of Sovereign's business processes. The TEAM philosophy became the cornerstone of the re-vitalised Sovereign culture and the benchmark for integrating new businesses into the Sovereign Group. The new structure Ballantyne created allowed Sovereign to handle the volume of work of a large company in the manner of a small company. Moreover, the changes Anderson made to the way broker development managers did their jobs, and the way they were remunerated, produced the needed sales growth. Overall, the internal revolution produced an even stronger company, superior levels of service and increased sales. Throughout it all, Sovereign continued to demonstrate its ability to re-invent New Zealand's life insurance industry and to set standards of service that its competitors would scramble to meet.

With all his years of experience, Hendry understood that it was not enough to have leading products and outstanding service, people had to know that you had them. Building the Sovereign brand was critical to the company's success, and he was a master at it.

CHAPTER 14
Building the Sovereign brand

"The lesson we learned from launching Sovereign is to start with a vision, articulate it, then communicate the hell out of it, which is precisely what we did."

Sovereign's overall success is, to a large extent, due to Hendry's achievement in building the Sovereign brand. The Sovereign brand may not be as well known as that of companies, such as AMP, who have been in the New Zealand market place for a long time, or of multi-nationals such as AXA or Royal & SunAlliance, but for a company started just over 12 years ago, the brand awareness throughout the general population is good. More importantly, the Sovereign brand is very well known and very positively viewed in the market that matters most, that of the independent adviser.

Building a brand from scratch is an interesting challenge. There is no shortage of textbooks describing how the task ought to be approached. Undertaking secondary research, primary research, creative testing, and developing and testing products and pricing, are some of essential activities in building a brand, in theory anyway. But in reality, it is often quite different. Entrepreneurs typically just get on and do it, relying on instincts and their own vision as the source of information and inspiration. So it was with Hendry. He had an unwavering belief that what Coon and he were planning to offer to the long-suffering New Zealand consumer was not just choice, but life insurance products that were significantly better. He also had a wealth of overseas experience in marketing within the financial services industry, and firsthand knowledge of launching products and services similar to those Sovereign would offer. On the downside, both he and Coon were new to the New Zealand market.

From the beginning Hendry had a clear plan of how the early Sovereign's initial products would be launched, followed by a more comprehensive range of protection, investment and mortgage products and services. Hendry was also very clear on Sovereign's distribution strategy, seeing Sovereign as the champion of independent brokers, that group of individuals who for whatever reason had not sold their souls to the major life companies. "This was all heady stuff," recalls Dwight Whitney who, along with his partner Kaye Coyne and former business partner Jane Berney, became the marketing consultants for Sovereign in 1988. "In hindsight it was slightly surrealistic as we sat in the borrowed rattan patio furniture in Chris and Ian's rented office," he recalls. "I'll always remember that office, and the energy and sense of belief these guys had. An English actuary with an unshakeable smile, a Scottish general manager with a marketing vision, a Canadian insurance salesman, and a vision of how they would launch a new financial services group in New Zealand."

"We were told January 3rd 1989 was to be the launch day, and that was that!"

One of Whitney and Coyne's first tasks was dealing with Hendry's impatience to get on with it. "It is often a compromise in the consulting business between doing things properly and getting things done," says Whitney. "From my academic and professional training, and certainly that of Kaye's, so much of Sovereign's launch was based on perception rather than concreteness. That made us feel uncomfortable to start with. It seemed to us risky to launch the company and its products without more information." In the early marketing meetings Whitney and Coyne would press Coon and Hendry. "Are you sure of your product positioning?" ... "Are you sure people will put their trust in a fledgling company run by two immigrants?" ... "Are you sure your distribution strategy is sound?" ... "Do you, in fact, know any of these so-called brokers waiting for liberation?" Each time the message came back loud and clear that the doing was more important than any unnecessary and timewasting analysis," says Whitney with a laugh. "We would be told we will launch first and then go through a process of more disciplined and more structured planning once the operation was underway. January 3rd 1989 was to be the launch day, and that was that!" And, of course, events proved Hendry right. Hendry knew he did not need to waste precious time analysing what the competition was doing or worrying about Sovereign's brand position vis à vis that of the other life companies because he and Coon had spent at least two years researching the New Zealand market and talking to brokers. "There wasn't really much need for formal research," Whitney admits, "because the market at that time featured very little differentiation in terms of competing brands, products or services. There were just the big players who were heavy, slow and complacent. Nobody seemed interested in developing new products or new ways of doing business." Hendry knew exactly what kind of company he wanted to build, and he had a clear picture of what he wanted the Sovereign brand to be. Therefore, he wanted Whitney's help in determining how this would best be done, particularly in light of the modest budget he had to work with.

The starting point for building the Sovereign brand was the development of the company logo, a symbol which they knew would become a key ingredient of the brand. This was developed by an Auckland graphic artist, David Bartlett, who had been Whitney's flatmate from university days. Bartlett had been hired to develop the Sovereign logo before Coyne and Whitney came on board. In fact, it was Bartlett who had recommended Whitney and Coyne to Coon and Hendry in the first place. Bartlett suggested the logo be a crest containing a mix of visual metaphors, consisting of very traditional financial services-type icons such as a pyramid and castle, the Southern Cross to reinforce the fact Sovereign was proudly a New Zealand company, and the flying eagle to represent the important connection with British-based Eagle Star. Both the logo and, indeed the Sovereign name itself, were designed to give the impression that Sovereign was a sound and reliable company while at the same time promoting the seemingly contradictory themes of Sovereign being state-of-the-art, entrepreneurial, innovative, flexible, service-driven and global in its outlook. The mix of metaphors was called quirky by some but that did not deter Hendry and Whitney. "I'm a strong believer that if you want to be perceived as being different, you have to act that way," says Whitney.

An important part of Sovereign's marketing success has been to develop one key document, which put into words and pictures the complicated messages that needed to be conveyed whenever a new initiative was launched. This touchstone set the tone both conceptually and creatively for all the other elements of the marketing campaign such as corporate literature, product literature and advertising material. These documents guided all management activity related to the new initiative and have helped to create a focus for all marketing activity, acting as blueprints for building the brand. The first of these touch stones was Sovereign's initial company profile. "This was a wonderful, powerful, colourful and creative document that would help successfully launch Sovereign, and subsequently get us all into a great deal of trouble," says Whitney. Few copies exist today as the Securities Commission ordered all copies destroyed. What got them into trouble were the words Hendry and Whitney used to describe Sovereign and its products. Their aim was to create a Camelot-like picture of Sovereign being a creative and positive company with a profound new sense of energy, but both now admit that the language they used to describe Sovereign, which included phrases such as 'the world's best,' was a bit excessive. "I have to admit, we made some pretty outrageous claims," says Hendry with a mischievous look in his eyes..

To avoid losing momentum after the company launch, Hendry immediately set about developing a marketing and communication strategic plan that would provide a continuing focus on building the Sovereign brand. The initial objectives of the plan were to position Sovereign among the upper echelon of insurance companies in New Zealand. Specifically, they wanted Sovereign to be viewed as:

- a leading, independent life assurance and superannuation company;
- offering a comprehensive range of investment assurance products and services modelled on internationally proven products;
- having strong affiliations with key international organisations by way of share-holding and other involvement;
- having skilled managers, proven leaders in the insurance investment markets;
- having an investment philosophy that combines the principles of strategic asset allocation and global diversification;
- having a product range that was available through an independent broker network;
- being a New Zealand-owned and operated organisation that is committed to New Zealanders' needs;
- providing a range of personal and business products covering home mortgages linked to the insurance plans, life insurance, disability income protection, investment assurance, and superannuation;
- being the company responsible for re-introducing the independent financial adviser/broker concept.

In the early days, much of the marketing activity relied on printed material, such as Sovereign's First Annual Review and the Sovereign Charter, which were designed to increase the company's profile and credibility. "Any advertising that we did was based on relatively meagre budgets," Whitney recalls. "But our advertising approach was always designed to be different from the norm. We were provocative and innovative, and we saw many an occasion where our competitors followed a creative path we had already travelled." Hendry and Whitney had fun creating images to convey some of the key marketing concepts they wished to communicate. For example, in one publication, lightning was used to convey Sovereign's 'shocking performance of success'. On other occasions, a globe was used to show Sovereign's business frame of reference; 'life turning upside down' was used to indicate that Sovereign's products would stop this from happening; a number of situations showed Sovereign to be a 'friend for life'; and rainbows were used to represent how the company's products would help people realise their dreams. Sovereign also received a letter about the rainbows, this time congratulating them on getting the range of colours in the right order. There was also a very adventurous multi-media campaign showing how Sovereign's customer service concept was one which treated you as a whole person.

Sovereign's strategy for media advertising has always been to spend small but look big. "We planned our media spend in such a way that it worked in combination with other media campaigns, such as our sponsored spots on 1ZB radio, and with ground signage. That way the perception was always that our spend was significantly greater than it actually was," says Whitney. "At crucial times, Sovereign appeared to be everywhere - or so we were told." One of the more successful activities for creating awareness of the Sovereign brand involved Sovereign's sponsorship of the 1ZB International Business Reports during the evening drive time. This was one of the first sponsored spots 1ZB introduced after their switch to a news/talk format, and the alignment with a credible source of business information helped to position Sovereign as an expert in financial and investment affairs. Developing a presence at nationally televised sporting events was another cost-effective way of raising Sovereign's profile. This was done through ground signage, a deal Whitney

> *Sovereign's strategy for media advertising has always been to spend small but look big.*

developed with Grant Fox who had hung up his rugby boots to become involved in sports marketing. Sovereign's involvement in New Zealand sport has been reinforced through sponsorship of the Auckland Rugby Union, the National Heart Foundation, the North Shore Hospice, the Wilson Home and many others. Another early marketing initiative was the development of guides, which told both advisers and policyholders about Sovereign's approach to such topics as risk management and investment. "This second tier of information packaging was important as both a sales tool and an adviser educational programme," says Whitney. "We were dealing with quite sophisticated insurance and investment concepts which were different from what most advisers were used to, and we had to go into quite a lot of detail to ensure both advisers and policy holders understood them."

> Excerpt from the first company profile
>
> Sovereign: powerful, unique, and state-of-the-art
>
> *For centuries, the word Sovereign has had a wide variety of positive symbols and interpretations.*
> *Sovereign, for example, can be:*
> – *A unique form of power.*
> – *A supreme ruler.*
> – *A good and effective influence.*
> – *A traditional gold coin.*
>
> *From 1989, the word Sovereign has a new meaning in the financial world.*
>
> *This definition is:*
> *An internationally-oriented and supported, New Zealand-based financial services company committed to offering competitive and innovative lifestyle-based products backed by a quality, customer driven philosophy and service.*

Hendry understood that the role of marketing was not just to project Sovereign's image and products, but also to learn about its customers and the marketplace in general. Thus the flow of information from marketing was from the outside in, too. "We also placed emphasis on gathering information both from intermediaries and clients," says Whitney. "A regular Sovereign broker audit which targeted those who did business with Sovereign, those who were thinking of it, and those who were adamantly against the idea, was not just an excellent public relations exercise, it proved Sovereign was listening. The information gave us important feedback about how well our distribution channel was working." This was not the only research undertaken by Sovereign. A pioneering study was conducted in conjunction with John Gandar of Research International to monitor how Sovereign's message was being interpreted in the marketplace by the general public. This research helped to clarify which product features were the most important to the buyer, and which messages were most effective.

Whitney's job of marketing Sovereign was made easier by the company's performance in the marketplace. "Sovereign's investment performance, initially, was nothing short of outstanding," says Whitney. "Sovereign consistently had the top, or near to the top, performing managed funds." These results could not have been more powerful and useful, coming as they did, in the early stages of Sovereign's life. Hendry and Whitney were quick to take advantage of Sovereign's performance excellence in a number of key promotions. Sovereign was voted the company independent advisers most preferred to deal with four times in the WA Taylor Industry Surveys. The first time this occurred, Hendry and Whitney wasted no time using these results in Sovereign's first TV campaign, and also in a print advertising campaign which crowed, "At Last An Industry Survey Puts Sovereign In Its Place". A framed copy of the print advertisement hangs on the wall in the reception area at Sovereign House to this day. The advertisement was also used in a direct mail campaign to advisers. Hendry and Coon were understandably proud of this achievement, as being Number 1 in the advisers' eyes was their main goal from the very beginning.

The role of marketing at Sovereign was not just to project the company's image and products, but also to learn about its customers and the marketplace in general.

A later television campaign focused on lifestyle themes. The first, code-named Cappuccino, showed two women talking over a cup of coffee about their investment or protection needs, and then discovering how they made the right decision by purchasing a Sovereign product. The second, code-named Tennis, was a scene in a locker room in a tennis club. The 'gun' player is insured with Sovereign whereas his less accomplished opponent is not. This advertisement was designed to make Sovereign seem desirable, progressive and sophisticated. This was later developed into a major magazine and press campaign. Sovereign also staged one of New Zealand's first nationally-linked non-broadcast television events for the launch of Sovereign's Superinvestor superannuation product range. This event involved a number of celebrities: Anita McNaught in her first corporate video; Tom Bradley as master of ceremonies; and Peter Eliot as the Man From The Future, extolling the virtues of Sovereign's new product. This event, more than any other, began the process of Sovereign coming out of its shell and being more on the front foot with its key audiences.

> *The aim was to develop corporate literature, which established a unique personality for Sovereign; material that was adventurous, humorous and different.*

Being different from the norm is one thing but looking different is another. Whitney and Coyne strove to develop corporate literature, which established a unique personality for Sovereign; material that was adventurous, humorous and different. "As with other elements of Sovereign's marketing mix," says Whitney, "we sought to be innovative and graphically adventurous in our material. Some have said our approach, at times, has been quirky, but the test for us has always been in putting our documents up against the competition. Consistently, Sovereign's stands out from rest." This did not always meet with a positive response, however. Whitney remembers the chameleon they developed for a new term life product called Adaptable Term. This was a more adaptable and value-added version of a straight life policy because it changed as the policyholder's life stage or situation changed. While the competition was going through a phase of high gloss, high people content for life policy literature at the time, Whitney and Coyne concentrated on providing graphic symbols to represent Sovereign's product. "Which is where the chameleon came in," recalls Whitney. "Ian must have been having a particularly bad day when we presented our creative recommendations for the product. He felt sure we were suggesting that Sovereign had become a 'scaly creature crawling up from the gutter.' He insisted we remove our adaptable lizard from his fine product, which we refused to do. The atmosphere was rather testy but Ian agreed to let lizard live, for the time being."

By 1997 Sovereign was a very different organisation to the one which had been launched eight years earlier. The one room office was now the multi-storied Sovereign House, and the rattan furniture had been replaced by leather, wood and pastel shades. The niche life company was by then a group made up of 90 entities, covering insurance, savings and investment products, financial planning services and asset management. A company that started with five key personnel, by 1997 employed over 400 people. In the early days, bringing a new adviser on board and gaining a presence in a new region was cause for celebration. By then, over 1,200 advisers throughout New Zealand chose to do business with Sovereign and recommended its products to their clients. In addition to this support from independent brokers, Sovereign had powerful distribution channels through subsidiary companies such as Caledonian Financial Services and Metropolitan Life. And, by 1997 the Annual Review had grown from 14 pages to 80. All of this spelled growth and development, and Whitney and Coyne believed it was time to review the Sovereign brand, and the direction they were taking. "It also felt like time for a change," says Whitney. "We argued, again from gut rather than from research, that the imagery that surrounded the old Sovereign symbol was no longer right for where the group was going." In Whitney's eyes, the Sovereign shield symbolised the old Sovereign, which was a life company, rather than the new financial services group. "We had, over time, been using the Sovereign symbol less and less for production," he recalls. It was cumbersome to reproduce and in a confined space it became the dominant element. It was more important for us to promote the Sovereign name than a logo element that had little meaning externally, or so we thought!"

Hendry agreed that the Sovereign logo needed updating. As with all strategic design development for Sovereign, Coyne and Whitney consulted with David Bartlett, the developer of the original Sovereign crest. Again, rather than do any market research, they went with their instincts of how they believed the new Sovereign should be portrayed. They were careful not to be too radical because many of the original Sovereign managers were reluctant to see the old Sovereign symbol go. The new symbol evolved from one of the original meanings of the word, sovereign, which was a coin. "We had any number of elements to work with," says Whitney, "because the eagle was no longer appropriate with the departure of Eagle Star, and the Tower was quickly eliminated because of the emergence of a competitor bearing the same name." The element they chose to develop was the ridges found on the edge of the Sovereign coin. This was formed into an ellipse, which was then modified further to become the Sovereign 'swoosh'. Bartlett also made subtle changes to the Sovereign typeface. The intention was to use the swoosh as the consistent element of the Sovereign brand. It would appear in all marketing material but the colour would be changed to represent the different entities, which now made up the larger financial services group, such as Sovereign Financial Services, Sovereign Assurance and Sovereign Fund Management. A regal blue and gold combination was reserved for the corporate entity.

To compliment the re-launching of the Sovereign brand, Whitney and Coyne developed a new advertising campaign which emphasised that Sovereign was a financial services group for the complete person. "Prior to developing this campaign," says Whitney, "we had done exhaustive research into all competitor material. The market at this time was considerably different to when Sovereign originally launched. There were more participants, greater diversity in products and services, and a much higher media profile among those claiming to be active in the broader financial services arena. But despite these changes, we found a great deal of similarity in creative execution among our competition. Again, our mantra said be different and we were." The re-launch campaign evolved around the creation of a central hero who, faced with a series of soul destroying encounters with an array of financial service providers, finds himself undergoing some quite dramatic physical changes which by the end leave him feeling decidedly less than whole. In fact, they were positively soul and body destroying. Using an extensive range of special effects, they then created a situation where, when he finally arrives at Sovereign, he finds himself whole again. The advertisements featured the tag line: Sovereign: The Financial Services Group For The Complete Person. The campaign included a 45 second television advertisement and also a four colour magazine advertisement that was initially designed to establish the broad business areas in which Sovereign now operated, such as risk management, investment

> *"We made a very real attempt to be and look different and in the end, the competition was forced to follow."*

and mortgages. A second phase of the campaign was developed to look specifically from the hero's perspective at the direct benefits of dealing with Sovereign for any of his other financial service needs.

Getting approval for the re-launch campaign was a little harder in 1997 than it had been at the time of the original launch in 1989 because there was now a board of directors to convince. "We focused our board presentation firstly on the reasons, as we saw them, for the change in the Sovereign brand," says Whitney. "We then took the board through a series of competitor television commercials before we showed them the proposed new look for Sovereign. It was, in hindsight, a rather risky strategy but having gained the prior approval of Ian Hendry we felt confident of board acceptance." With only one exception, the board was pleased with the new advertising campaign. Chairman Bruce Bornholdt, in particular, took great pleasure in seeing the advertisement played. The euphoria, however, was short lived for within a few months Hendry ordered the campaign pulled. "Hendry's decision to pull the campaign so quickly was surprising given the approval from the top," says Whitney. "Although Ian was still the prime decision maker he was now being influenced by a wider range of people wanting a greater say in matters they believed fell into their domain." Some lobbied Hendry to kill the campaign because they felt the new image did not represent the company in the way they believed it should be represented; whereas others objected because they had been left out of the process.

In spite of such hiccups, Hendry, Coyne and Whitney achieved a great deal with a small budget. In a very short period of time, they played a key role in taking an unknown start-up company to the position of having twice the market share of its nearest competitor. The secrets of Sovereign's marketing success were setting very high quality standards, and being consistent in their messages and communications. But most importantly, they were not afraid to be unique. "We made a very real attempt to be and look different," says Whitney. "In text, graphic treatment, advertising and other areas of physical evidence, we consciously differed from the norm and from expectations. In the end, the competition was forced to follow."

CHAPTER 15

The MetLife purchase: a giant step forward

"Sovereign Scores MetLife Prior To Listing"
The New Zealand Herald

With the Securities Commission held at bay, Eagle Star off their backs, and the internal revolution under way, Coon and Hendry began the task of re-positioning Sovereign. Even as early as 1989 they had talked about Sovereign becoming a world class financial services company, and by the mid 1990s the time was right to make it happen. But by the mid 1990s this was now a very challenging task. The marketplace was complex and fast changing, and there was greater competition, due to the convergence of the insurance and banking industries. In addition, the established life companies, still Sovereign's main competitors, had lifted their game and were delivering better service, offering a wider range of customer-friendly products, and were generally operating more efficiently. Even after Sovereign's impressive early success, there were many who doubted that it would ever become anything more than a niche life insurance company. Not only had Coon and Hendry succeeded in creating a world-class financial services group, but they had achieved it with staggering speed. It took only six years for Sovereign to go from five staff and two products, to having hundreds of staff and a full compliment of products in the areas of risk, investment, mortgage and superannuation.

By 1995, Sovereign was hungry for growth. Coon and Hendry saw both the need, and the marketplace opportunity, for Sovereign to provide a variety of financial services such as mortgages and superannuation products. The need existed because becoming larger was Sovereign's main defence against being taken over. The opportunities existed because by moving away from being a single product company to a multi-service group, the company could produce greater efficiencies and profits. Becoming a financial services group would also allow Sovereign to develop a wider range of distribution channels, and therefore to tap into different markets having an even wider range of needs. Coon and Hendry believed Sovereign could do this without jeopardising its relationships with the independent brokers that they had worked so hard to develop. They were convinced that a broader financial services base would make Sovereign more stable and more dynamic, and would offer the company the ability to achieve the growth they desired.

The transition from a small niche business to a larger, more diversified corporate is difficult to manage because during this period the company is quite vulnerable to a take-over bid. While Sovereign's organic growth had always been more than satisfactory, it was not sufficient to provide the company with the necessary horsepower to move it out of the danger area. Therefore, to protect itself Sovereign needed to acquire another established business, and by the mid 1990s Coon and Hendry were searching for a company to take over. There was a second reason for acquiring a profitable business, and that had to do with taxation issues. "Because of the way life offices are taxed, Sovereign had accumulated huge tax losses in its early years despite making operating profits," says Hendry, "so we were looking to acquire a company that had taxable profits so we could frank our losses."

Coon and Hendry's first choice was Guardian Assurance. They had a number of discussions with Guardian's owners but they could not agree on the worth of the company. "We were going to form a joint company and the major issue was how much of it would we own and how much they would own," says Coon. "Guardian's directors had this interesting way of calculating the company's value and they thought their company was worth twice what we thought it was. We said, okay, we'll calculate Sovereign's worth on the same basis, but that produced a ridiculously high value for Sovereign which they didn't like very much." Not optimistic about being able to negotiate a deal, in 1995 Coon and Hendry turned their attentions instead to buying Metropolitan Life. As it turned out, Guardian was back on the market in 1998 but by then Sovereign could not afford it. "It was just before our public listing and the timing was not right," says Hendry. Guardian was eventually sold to Royal & SunAlliance.

The first choice was Guardian.

Metropolitan Life, known in the industry as MetLife, was founded in 1962 by a group of Auckland professional people, led by lawyer Don St Clair Brown, who believed that their own clients were not being well served by the existing life companies. Known in the beginning as the Auckland Life Insurance Company, its initial focus was on providing property investment and life assurance products. "Like Sovereign, MetLife focused on the needs of the policyholders," says Peter Fitzsimmons, who joined the company in 1981 as marketing manager, and who later became managing director. "We were very customer focused and very popular as a result. The company especially looked after young New Zealanders who were purchasing their first homes." MetLife soon developed a reputation for product innovation. It was, for example, the first company in New Zealand to offer a non-smoker discount, and this later evolved into a good health bonus. The company also positioned itself as being good corporate citizens by sponsoring youth yachting and youth athletics.

MetLife grew rapidly, first using independent brokers as Sovereign had done, and then establishing its own tied agency force with branch offices throughout New Zealand. It built a substantial money lending book and an impressive portfolio of commercial property investments. By the 1970s, the company, now called Metropolitan Life, was well established. Unfortunately, MetLife was also in that vulnerable position of being between a niche player and a diversified corporate, and over the next ten years, it went through various changes in ownership. This included a public listing on the New Zealand share market in 1987, until in 1988, the company fell under the control of the Australian insurance company, FAI. "Under FAI, the company became very focused on profit and on being run efficiently," says Fitzsimmons. "By the mid 90s we, like Sovereign, were looking for opportunities to grow. We knew it couldn't be done organically so we had to acquire or be acquired."

Sovereign's first approach to FAI to explore purchasing MetLife was through David Belcher of Clavell Investments. He had represented FAI when they listed the Newmarket Property Trust on the NZSE, and therefore had developed a relationship with Dr Frank Wolf and Rodney Adler, both key figures in FAI. Belcher first approached Adler with the suggestion that Sovereign might be interested in purchasing MetLife. Adler had mixed feelings about the suggestion. On the one hand, he had met Coon and Hendry before and had been impressed with Sovereign. "He had been very flattering about Sovereign's performance," says Hendry, "and often wondered out loud why MetLife couldn't achieve the same growth." But Adler also had some reservations. "There was a great deal of scepticism on FAI's part on whether Sovereign had the resources to complete the transaction," says Eric Bachmann, who as Sovereign's long-time lawyer was in the middle of the negotiations.

The negotiations were difficult, the most difficult, in fact, that Hendry, Coon or Bachmann had ever been involved in. "These people were difficult to deal with, and that's the understatement of the century," says Hendry. "They were very aggressive and drove a hard bargain. And, everything had to be complex. They had a habit of throwing in complex issues at the last minute." Apart from the personalities of Adler and Wolf, two factors made reaching agreement difficult. The first was how they valued MetLife. "They had a $90 million company that they thought was worth $125 million," says Coon in his usual direct style. The second was the complexity of the structure of MetLife with its two listed companies and numerous relationships with other businesses. "The trouble with the deal," says Bachmann, "was that there were about ten side deals hanging off it. We had to work our way through all sorts of other investment arrangements that FAI had entered into."

Final negotiations took six weeks and came to a head on March 7, 1996 at 7am in Bachmann's offices at Hesketh Henry. For a variety of complex reasons relating to the need to give adequate notice to shareholders, an agreement had to be reached by midnight that day if the deal was to proceed. "It was chaos," says Bachmann. "The entire 11th floor of our offices was occupied by 20 people involved in the negotiations. Anybody who had anything to do with the transaction was there." To complicate matters further, in addition to those gathered in Hesketh Henry's offices, there were two lots of lawyers in Australia, one acting for FAI and one for Sovereign, who along with Adler and Wolf were negotiating from their offices in Sydney. All day long offers and counter offers were hurled back and forth between the parties and across the Tasman. The negotiations tested Coon and Hendry's mettle. "Frank Wolf was a brilliant negotiator," says Hendry. "He could think his way through very complex deals. We often thought he was two steps ahead of us." Of course, Wolf had the advantage of knowing the intricacies of the MetLife structure while Coon, Hendry and Bachmann had to discover them as the deal unfolded. At one point, Wolf faxed through a formula for handling the early easement of a loan. "The trouble was that no one at Sovereign could understand any part of it," says Bachmann laughing. Meanwhile, MetLife's officers, such as Peter Fitzsimmons, had to wait at Hesketh Henry's offices all night, just in case they were required to sign key documents relating to the sale.

The original 4PM deadline for signing the agreement came and went. At 10PM some of the major shareholders of Metlifecare, a subsidiary of MetLife, showed up with two barristers in an attempt to stop the deal from proceeding. At 11:45PM, without the deal having been concluded, Hendry rushed back to Sovereign's head office to fax Sovereign's shareholders so they could comply with the midnight deadline for giving notice of the impending purchase. As negotiations continued into the night, the atmosphere became very tense and at times tempers became frayed. There were several times when it looked as if the deal would collapse. At one point, in the early hours of the morning, Bachmann's phone rang. He pressed the speaker button so that everyone present could hear his wife say, "So, you are still alive." Finally, at 4am, the deal was signed. It was a great moment for Sovereign. The deal with MetLife doubled the company's size with the stroke of a pen and established Sovereign as a major financial services company. "MetLife gave us a critical mass and a profile that we could not have achieved through organic growth alone," says Hendry. "Sovereign became a major life insurance company as a result." But by 4AM, everyone was too tired to go out and celebrate. "The deal killed my secretary," says Bachmann with a grin. "She had insisted on working the entire 21 hours it took to complete the deal but she retired with Occupational Stress Syndrome shortly afterwards."

When Sovereign purchased MetLife in 1996, MetLife's portfolio of products included life and disability insurance protection, personal superannuation and mortgages. More importantly, Sovereign was instantly able to add 80,000 new clients, annual premium sales of $7,816,000, single premium sales of $25,883,000 and in-force annual premiums of $43,993,000 to its financial profile. Through the purchase, Sovereign also achieved a number of its strategic objectives. The group was now one of the largest New Zealand life insurers in terms of premium revenue, and had both the size and the stature to be a major player in the financial services industry. Not surprisingly, the acquisition by the youngster Sovereign of a company formed in 1962 was big news in the New Zealand marketplace. The New Zealand Herald ran a story headed "Sovereign Scores MetLife Prior To Listing" and the article described the purchase as providing "a solid platform from which to build on its core business and expand in related areas of the financial services sector such as home mortgages, regular savings, superannuation and retirement care."

As several banks in New Zealand have discovered in recent years, it is one thing to acquire another company, and it is another to merge the two companies into one efficient operating unit. The project to amalgamate Sovereign and MetLife was headed by Hendry with the major responsibility for implementation being given to Ballantyne. The omens for a successful merger were good. Hendry and Ballantyne had a clear picture of what the enlarged company's operating style had to be. Furthermore, Ballantyne and her team had prior experience managing change within Sovereign and, therefore, had some idea of what the issues and pitfalls would be. It also helped that the people at MetLife were positive about the takeover. "People at MetLife were used to change because we had had six changes of ownership in a decade," says Fitzsimmons. "Also people could see that becoming part of Sovereign presented them with wonderful opportunities." Most importantly, there was a good fit between the philosophy and values of the two organisations. In spite of this promising start, people at Sovereign were realistic enough to know the successful integration of the two companies would not happen overnight. Accordingly, Hendry gave Ballantyne one year to complete the merger.

Of all the projects undertaken during Sovereign's growth spurt, the merger with MetLife was the most successful, the most well managed, and the one truest to the company's guiding philosophies and style. It was not a case of the conquered and the vanquished. Instead, a great deal of care was taken to treat MetLife staff well. "It is a good case study of how to handle a merger," says Fitzsimmons. "People were impressed by Sovereign's openness and sensitivity to the human factors. In the end, only a handful of MetLife staff chose not to move to Sovereign." The fact that the merger was handled by Ballantyne, custodian of the Sovereign culture, is the major reason why the merger was so successful. Her people skills, excellent organisational abilities and her talent for communicating the core values of the Sovereign culture were invaluable in bringing MetLife into the Sovereign fold. "Naomi made sure there was compassionate treatment of the MetLife staff," says Anderson. "But the best part was communication. She made sure that everyone in both companies knew what was going on."

> *The strategy for merging the companies was simple.*

The strategy for merging the companies was simple. Key MetLife management were quickly identified and given positions within

Sovereign. Very wisely, particularly given his influence within the company, Sovereign maintained Peter Fitzsimmons' position as managing director of MetLife. In every way, Fitzsimmons was Mr MetLife. He commanded huge loyalty and respect from his staff, and therefore his support was critical in ensuring the MetLife distribution arm would remain intact. If he had resigned, panic might well have set in among the tied agency force, causing them to desert and join the security of one of Sovereign's competitors. Fitzsimmons also had a wealth of experience and a great deal of credibility in the life industry. Persuading Fitzsimmons to become part of Sovereign sent out the right signals to the marketplace. Moreover, his expertise was an asset from which Sovereign benefited greatly.

The merger was not without irony. Coon and Hendry had always rejected the notion of having a tied agency force and now they had gone and bought one! The challenge they now faced was to manage this group effectively so they would continue to perform well in an organisation that was focused primarily on working with independent advisers. Hendry decided to put long-time stalwart and original shareholder, Ernie Uganecz, into MetLife to work with its agents. If Ballantyne was the keeper of the culture within Sovereign, Uganecz was its biggest exponent to the outside world. "Ernie carries the fire and the passion of Sovereign," says David Anderson. "He is a great communicator of what Sovereign is all about." Indeed, Uganecz enjoyed nothing more than standing in front of a group of independent brokers, and preaching the gospel according to Sovereign. The consummate insurance salesman, he could sell ice to the Eskimos. The more sceptical his audience, the more passionate and persistent he would become. The MetLife move gave Uganecz a new challenge, and a wonderful opportunity to shepherd more unbelievers into the Sovereign fold. It also gave Hendry a loyal supporter who could help monitor how the absorption of the MetLife sales force was progressing.

Merging the administrative functions of the two companies posed the greatest challenge. A transition management team headed by Ballantyne set up residence in MetLife's Parnell offices and began the task of moving the administrative functions to Takapuna where Sovereign's more modern systems would result in increased efficiencies. Ballantyne and her team also developed a number of key performance indicators for the merger. These were largely based on the TQM foundations that Sovereign itself had established in the internal revolution. As well as looking at how multi-skilling and the TEAM process would work among MetLife staff, Ballantyne also spent a lot of time merging the two company cultures into one. This involved one-to-one meetings with staff to discuss her strategy, goals and the Sovereign culture, training courses for MetLife staff to learn new skills, constant communication to keep staff informed and a number of staff social events where the two tribes could interact and get to know one another.

The merger of the two companies had to be managed in the outside world as well. The decision was made to maintain the MetLife brand for existing policyholders in the short-term, but the long-term strategy was to introduce MetLife customers to the wider range of Sovereign products and services now available to them. Similarly, it was decided to allow the MetLife agents to continue to work under the MetLife brand in the short-term but later to transform them into a distribution arm of the expanded Sovereign Group. As it happened, Uganecz and Fitzsimmons did such a good job of selling Sovereign that the pressure to become Sovereign agents came from the MetLife agents themselves.

To mark the acquisition, a special newsletter called New Horizons, which was a synthesis of Sovereign's Sovereign News and Met Life's Thinking Ahead publications, was sent to all policyholders in June, 1996. The publication was upbeat, positive, glossy, and bullish. Policyholders were told that the move to buy MetLife marked "the start of a new era for financial service in New Zealand," and that the new entity was clearly "in the first division of life insurers in New Zealand."

With the MetLife purchase, Sovereign was now indeed a major player in the New Zealand financial services industry. It had become one of the largest life offices in the country. That Sovereign had been able to orchestrate the purchase at all, and that it was able to attract significant capital from some blue chip overseas investors to fund the purchase, helped further silence Sovereign's few remaining detractors. Moreover, that Sovereign had been able to transplant its original vision, values and culture so easily into the MetLife organisation showed there was still power and validity in those original beliefs.

But the MetLife merger was not the only initiative to occupy Coon and Hendry's attention. In 1996, they decided it was time to get back into the home mortgage business, and like everything at Sovereign, they did it big time.

CHAPTER 16

Home mortgages: another great success

"We have introduced a lot of traditional life insurance brokers to the world of mortgage lending. This has created a new market for them and broadened our channels for distributing mortgage products."

Coon and Hendry had always intended that Sovereign be a major player in the home lending market. Mortgages had been part of Sovereign's original product mix with the launch of HomePlan 1000. In the beginning, funding was provided by the National Australia Bank (NAB). Unlike its competitors, the bank had agreed to charge no fees and also offered a very attractive rate of interest. This gave Sovereign a competitive advantage which when coupled with the other features of Homeplan 1000 made the product very popular. But then Sovereign's main contact at NAB left and his replacement was less enthusiastic about the arrangement. The problem was that through HomePlan 1000, Sovereign was offering interest only mortgages with the principal sum being repaid only when the policy matured. The new man, who had come from the bank's Australian operation, saw how much money was being lent to homeowners through HomePlan 1000, saw that no principal was being repaid, and became nervous. When he saw how small and new Sovereign was, he became extremely nervous. Deciding that the bank was too exposed, he cancelled, almost overnight, NAB's arrangement with Sovereign. "That was pretty much the death-knell for HomePlan 1000," says Hendry. "Although we found other banks that would provide funding, no one would give us such a competitive rate as NAB did." Sales declined as a result, and some years later HomePlan1000 was withdrawn from the market.

Coon and Hendry were eager to get back into the mortgage business because once a mortgage was sold, it provided an opportunity to on-sell a full array of insurance and investment products. They could also see that non-bank mortgage finance was becoming big business across the Tasman. Brands such as Aussie Home Loans, for example, were reaping the rewards of a trend, which by 1997 saw 15% of secured housing finance business going to non-banks. By 1997, a number of non-bank entities were starting to emerge in New Zealand and there was a small mortgage broking fraternity already in existence. The mortgage business by then was worth in excess of $48.1 billion. Sovereign decided to enter that market and in Coon and Hendry style, they set their eyes on becoming the leader in this new area. But the problem of finding a reliable source of funding at a competitive rate still remained.

The solution was for Sovereign to raise its own funds through securitisation. In simple terms, securitisation is the process whereby a large number of individual assets, such as home mortgages, are packaged together in a special purpose investment vehicle with interests in that vehicle being sold to one or more third parties. The key benefit of securitisation is access to funds at a rate that, when offered as a mortgage, is competitive with that provided by banks. Following the MetLife acquisition, Sovereign had the standing to attract the significant funding this new venture would require. Coon and Hendry held discussions with a number of financial institutions, eventually teaming up with Deutsche Bank. "Sovereign was the first life company to use securitisation in its full form," says Hendry. "In fact, until quite recently we were the only life office to use it." As a result, Sovereign developed a reputation for being experts in this type of financing. Altogether, Sovereign has launched five tranches of mortgage-backed bonds through Deutsche Bank and Westpac. "These have been very successful," Hendry says with pride. "Sovereign paper is seen as having value in the marketplace." The arrangement has been a win-win for both parties. Having the support of high profile organisations such as Deutsche Bank and Westpac gave credibility to Sovereign's new mortgage venture and by working with Sovereign, Deutsche Bank has been able to break into new markets.

Today, Sovereign is the largest non-bank provider of home lending.

In order to manage an expanding mortgage business, in 1995 Coon and Hendry created a stand-alone organisation called Sovereign Financial Services (SFS), which was run by Paul Bravo. SFS also looked after a subsidiary company called S H Lock, which had formerly been part of the Findlay Group of companies, the second oldest listed company on the British stock exchange. Lock, in its own right, had been in business for over a century and had been an active player in the trade finance market in New Zealand since the 1950s. The idea to acquire S H Lock arose during the course of a luncheon between Hendry and Lock's managing director, Leslie Jacques, at Auckland's Northern Club. While trade finance at that time could hardly be described as core business for Sovereign, the combination of Lock's heritage and profitability made the acquisition all the more attractive. Hendry also thought the acquisition of Lock would bring Sovereign some experience in managing a lending operation.

Hendry did not want to establish a new distribution system to sell Sovereign's mortgage products. He believed that Sovereign's existing adviser network, which had been enthusiastic about HomePlan 1000, would be receptive to the new product. In addition, he believed the mortgage broking network would be attracted to products backed by Sovereign's service orientation, as long as the interest rate was competitive. In 1996, Sovereign Home Mortgages Limited was established to provide the day-to-day management of mortgage finance distribution. Sovereign also put significant resources behind a fledgling mortgage distribution company called New Zealand Home Loans, a business established by a life broker, and his business partner, who had strong Sovereign connections. Sovereign also formed a strategic alliance with The Public Trust to market its mortgage products.

Under the mantle of *Sovereign, The Home of Mortgages*, Sovereign re-entered the mortgage market in 1996, and within a very short period of time had a mortgage book of $100 million. The portfolio included two products: Manager Plus which was a table mortgage with both floating and fixed rate options as well as a redraw facility on the floating component, and Access Plus which was a table mortgage which combined a revolving credit facility with a floating interest rate. Added to these was Freehold, a mortgage protection insurance package combining death, disability or critical illness protection. The launch was an immediate success with sales exceeding all expectations.

Sovereign's mortgage business has never looked back. Today, Sovereign is the largest non-bank provider of home lending. "What is really pleasing," says Hendry, "is that we have introduced a lot of traditional life insurance brokers to the world of mortgage lending. This has created a new market for them and broadened our channels for distributing mortgage products."

But while the acquisition of MetLife and the growth of the home mortgage business were two giant steps forward for Sovereign, another venture was not going so well. Business, it seems, is often two steps forward and one step back.

CHAPTER 17

New Zealand Superannuation Services: one small step back

"If you fail to prepare for your future, prepare to fail in having the lifestyle you want."

One initiative which had a less successful outcome was Sovereign's attempt to direct market personal superannuation products. It frustrated Sovereign's management no end that more people were not placing their investment money with the company, particularly in the days of Sovereign's early success when the company was consistently the top performer in managed funds. They understood that Sovereign's youth was always an issue and that the market was wary of so-called new high flyers, especially after the 1989 crash, but on the back of Sovereign's consistent investment performance, the management team believed that common sense would prevail and Sovereign would receive the support it deserved. Also, since the country's politicians were making noises about the possible demise of the National Super scheme, they believed that the market would be receptive to a more tailored superannuation-type product. The time was right, the team decided, for Sovereign to introduce a new superannuation product into the market.

Sovereign's first product offering had been a comprehensive group of products marketed under the Superinvestor range. The launch of this new offering in 1991 was one of Sovereign's grandest ever. It was stunning. With then national newsreader Tom Bradley as the master of ceremonies, the event was staged from the ballroom at Auckland's Sheraton Hotel, which, at the time, was the pre-eminent New Zealand hotel property. The decision was made to base the event in Auckland because that is where the majority of advisers whom Sovereign wanted to impress were based. But in a first for any New Zealand company, a live simulcast was beamed to locations throughout the country. The production was, in fact, one of the first for Moving Pictures, the recently created outside broadcast facility for TVNZ. Because the event was as much a celebration of Sovereign's success as it was a new product launch, Coon and Hendry commissioned a pseudo-documentary of the Sovereign story to date which was fronted by TV personality, Anita McNaught. Another talent on the rise, it was the first such corporate video that McNaught had taken part in. It featured interviews with Coon, Hendry, and Arun Abey, as well as some well-scripted editorial by McNaught outlining the company's meteoric success. The theme of the launch was travelling into outer space and off into the future. The production ended with a return to earth by the Man from the Future in the form of Gloss star and TV heartthrob Peter Elliot. Elliot had been picked because of his name and star qualities but he also was one of the earliest Superannuation policyholders. Thanks to the set designers from TVNZ, a spaceship full of special effects landed on the stage at the Sheraton. From this craft Elliot emerged with tales from the future: how bleak it was for some, but how marvellous it was for him because in 1991 he had taken out a Superinvestor policy. Following Elliot's introduction, a 20-minute video was screened, again starring Elliot, and directed by Tony Holden, the man who later would make his name as the director of Shortland Street. The audience was stunned. The event was without question the most sophisticated and extravagant product launch they had ever seen, and the industry buzzed about it for months afterwards. But Superinvestor failed to achieve the sales volumes Hendry had hoped for.

Despite some tinkering with the product, some re-branding, and the creation of more targeted offerings such as a bond product and a product tailored to the executive market, Superinvestor never achieve the level of sales that Hendry wanted. Politically, however, the subject of retirement planning and of the need for people to take control of their own financial future was gaining momentum. It had, through the efforts of Winston Peters, become a national issue and would soon become the subject of a referendum. Convinced there was a market for superannuation products in New Zealand, Hendry refused to give up, and he believed that the cause of the problem of poor sales was in distribution. "I was convinced that existing strategies and distribution solutions were not working," he says. "I thought we needed to develop a specialist channel that was totally focused on superannuation products." This line of thinking was sound. Most brokers at the time were specialising in selling risk products with investment products being sold by financial

"I was convinced that existing strategies and distribution solutions were not working."

planners. Thus, the majority of the independent advisers selling Sovereign's products would not be focusing on selling Superinvestor. Unfortunately, this line of thinking also led Sovereign management to make a big mistake. In 1996 Sovereign created New Zealand Superannuation Services (NZSS).

Hendry appointed Craig Abel to head NZSS. Abel, an American from Okalahoma, had cut his sales teeth as a time-share salesman, first in the USA, then in Israel, and later throughout South Africa, before finally ending up in New Zealand with Prudential. Along the way he had collected a handful of associates who formed the management of the new company. They always travelled in a group. The joke soon went around Sovereign that if you were having a meeting with Abel, you had better bring another 5 chairs. When Hendry met them, Abel and his team had been the superannuation sales arm of Prudential Insurance. They were very successful in making sales but they were also making waves. Much of what they were doing within Prudential was seen by the industry as being a bit suspect. Hendry and Whitney positioned the brand of NZSS to look very much like a government department, that is to say, stable, conservative, and established. Unfortunately, the sales approach taken by Abel and his colleagues appears to have been inconsistent with this image. Their style was the hard sell tactics of the time-share or used car industries: lure them, seduce them, scare them, snare them and lock them in.

The marketing strategy was for NZSS to be Auckland based and then later rolled out around the major population centres of New Zealand. Thus, the NZSS headquarters were positioned in the heart of the fashionable Auckland retail suburb of Newmarket, adjacent to a mall development, which was being created under the mantle of one of MetLife's arms, the Newmarket Property Trust. The mall would serve as part of the lure. Under the direction of one of New Zealand's larger specialist direct marketing agencies, a TV event was produced to both develop the NZSS brand and to drive a direct response campaign. It was the most flamboyant and costly endeavour in Sovereign's history, surpassing even the 1991 product launch. Perhaps inspired by the character from the original Superinvestor launch, the creative team latched onto the concept of a person from the future reporting on the need to save. Rather than going down the less ambitious route of creating their own character, project director, Rob Davis, decided to feature Dr Who, the ultimate time-traveller. The idea mesmerised everyone at Sovereign. Even normally financially cautious people like

Hendry and Ballantyne fell in love with the concept, and where before dollars had always been an issue in making marketing decisions, suddenly they were not. Following sustained negotiations with the BBC, Sovereign bought the rights to use the Dr Who character as well as the Tardis device, around which the direct response element of the campaign would work. One of the original, and still surviving, Dr Who actors was found and jetted first class to Auckland. His arrival made the evening news and was a cause for celebration among the Dr Who Fan Club. A complete Dr Who set was created in the studios of the recently defunct Aotearoa Broadcasting. This included his Time Travelling machine, his headquarters, and of course the Tardis. In mid summer, Dr Who donned his enormous overcoat and related paraphernalia and a series of television commercials were made at both indoor and outdoor locations. The value proposition for NZSS was identical to the original creative theme employed at the Superinvestor launch in 1991: if you fail to prepare for your future, prepare to fail in having the lifestyle you want. It is true that this is a bleak outlook, the message said, but one that can be avoided merely by phoning 0800 Tardis and speaking to people at NZSS who are there to help. By ringing this number the caller would be put in touch with an NZSS consultant who would then make an appointment to meet them.

At the same time as the Dr Who campaign was launched, another strategy for attracting customers was being implemented which was truly shades of time-share selling. A brochure was distributed around Auckland's more affluent suburbs that promised the bearer $100 worth of goods or services from designated retailers if they would simply come into the NZSS offices for a chat. The brochure included a replica of a $100 bill, and all people needed to do to have it authorised as 'legal tender' was to come in for the interview. The phones went crazy and NZSS was under way.

The NZSS offices were designed with the sales process firmly in mind. There was a comfortable greeting and assembly area where the prospective customer would come at a pre-agreed time. Once the pleasantries were over, the NZSS salesperson would take the prospect into a specially designed chamber of horrors showing the consequences of failing to plan for retirement. Once they left the chamber, the prospects were moved to an area full of desks where the sales pitch went into full swing. If the salesperson could not close the sale, he went to get his superior who subjected the prospect to an even harder sell. If that failed, the prospect was reluctantly allowed to leave. Some did maintain their resistance and were given an endorsement for their $100. Many people signed up for a policy due to the very persuasive tactics of the sales force. It was, in the eyes of the NZSS crew, purely a numbers game but one without any quality control, or any concern for the persistency of the business written. It was not the Sovereign way of doing things.

> *At one stage, NZSS resorted to using the telephone book to identify prospects.*

What the management team had not realised was that the waters NZSS was trawling for prospects had already been largely plundered during Abel's time at Prudential. Thus the NZSS fishing expedition was not producing the number of leads that were expected. At one stage, NZSS resorted to using the telephone book to identify prospects but eventually it gave that up when it was discovered to be a very inefficient way of attracting leads. Furthermore, those that it did produce were often unsuited to the product NZSS was trying to sell. Even more disappointingly, there was no more success with the Dr Who advertising campaign than with the phone book. While the Dr Who concept looked good in theory, the reality was that much of the target audience had no idea who the character was. Despite all the promises and projections the sales figures were not stacking up.

As things progressed from bad to worse, Sovereign came under attack from a number of quarters. The industry, in particular, queried the ethics of having such an important subject as saving for your retirement treated in such a trivial way. With the Securities Commission still keeping a watchful eye on Sovereign, this scrutiny was the last thing Coon and Hendry needed. Soon after, Fair Go got wind of NZSS and both the company and promotional campaign featured as the lead item on the show. "We all watched with horror as the fiasco unfolded," says Coon. Hendry and his team reacted quickly. It is not part of the Sovereign culture to blame people for an error, therefore people do not attempt to to deny or cover up mistakes instead to face up to them and to act quickly to correct them. Hendry took full responsibility for the failure of the NZSS, although launching NZSS had been a team decision. He very quickly started putting things right. Abel and his men were dismissed, the Newmarket house of horrors was shut down, and New Zealand Superannuation Services was brought back into head office, and very quietly allowed to die.

But the worst part of the NZSS debacle was the impact it was having on the company's most important source of business, its adviser network. Though Sovereign was still claiming to be the champion of the independent adviser, the perception of many was that, by establishing NZSS, Sovereign had set up their own distribution company, which was in direct competition with the adviser network, and in a high profile way at that. Sovereign lost an enormous amount of good will and credibility as a result. NZSS was not the only reason advisers were starting to turn away from Sovereign. Service standards were starting to slip and a number of loyal brokers who had championed Sovereign from the early days were starting to become disgruntled. One, Jane Butler, became so frustrated with Sovereign that she drastically reduced the new business she wrote with them. Butler experienced a number of service failures which had serious implications for her clients or her business, but the straw that broke the camel's back was when she got a request for feedback signed, 'The Operations Department.' Butler completed the form and wrote on the bottom, 'please don't become another faceless organisation. You started out leaving everyone else standing in the dust.' One of the service failures that Butler experienced involved a policy that was ready to be issued but was delayed for no apparent reason for two months. "It took several faxes and phone calls, and then contact with Errol Timmins, the underwriter, before the policy was issued," she says. "It was just so disappointing to be working with a company that had been exceptional in every sense, and in just a period of three years had fallen so far short in so many areas."

Why was Sovereign struggling to maintain service standards? One problem was rapid growth. The company had become large so quickly in so many different areas making it hard for Hendry to keep on top of what was going on in the company. There was also the problem of the conflict between Anderson and Ballantyne. But one problem over-shadowed the rest.

It was payback time.

CHAPTER 18
Going public at last

What Coon and Hendry did not realise was how tortuous the path to a public listing would be, what toll it would take both on them personally and on the business, and how little would result from their efforts.

Apart from the small hiccup of New Zealand Superannuation Services, Sovereign's success was outstripping all expectations. 1996 was a particularly successful year with the MetLife purchase and Sovereign's successful re-entry into the home mortgages market. But one old problem was still haunting Coon and Hendry. The need for more capital would not go away. "It was list or sell," says Coon, "so the decision was made to try again to list on the NZSE." In preparation for this second attempt, investment broker David Belcher was appointed as an adviser to the board. Eventually, prior to Sovereign's public listing, he became a full board member. Belcher's firm, Clavell Capital teamed up with JB Were for the second listing, and the process of due diligence began in 1997.

Once again the listing process was arduous and consumed a tremendous amount of Coon and Hendry's time and energy, as well as that of Coon's brother, Richard. As Sovereign's chief financial officer, he was in the thick of strategic planning and negotiating with overseas investors. There were countless meetings involving most of the key people within the Sovereign organisation. In addition, there were strategy sessions, overseas trips to persuade international investors, and road shows around New Zealand explaining the listing to the investment community. The result of all this activity was the same as it had been 1994: it took Hendry's focus away from key internal and local business issues. Sovereign paid a big price as a result, which is exactly what he feared would happen. To make matters worse, the listing was an on-again off-again affair. The listing date was postponed several times over a twelve-month period until finally someone had the courage to say 'damn the torpedoes and full speed ahead.' By the end of 1997 the strain was evident on Coon and

Hendry's faces. They looked tired and stressed, a far cry from the irrepressible optimists who teamed up in 1988 to turn their dream into reality.

In the second attempt to go public, the strategy was to actively and aggressively market shares to a series of institutional investors, both in New Zealand and overseas, in an attempt to avoid the problem that occurred in the first IPO where Sovereign's competitors stalled the listing by refusing to participate in the share float. This strategy was quite successful in attracting offshore investment houses, such as Eldon Capital, an American company who purchased a large parcel of shares in return for having a director on Sovereign's board. But once again, there was little support from local institutions. Hendry tried to be unconcerned by this. He continued to believe that once the listing had gone through and Sovereign was in the NZSE 40, the local institutions would be forced to buy Sovereign shares to maintain a balanced portfolio. Although the listing went through on April 3rd, 1998, the local investment houses continued to ignore Sovereign. As a result there was no local market for the company's shares.

Sovereign's share price languished because there was no interest from the local investment houses, which were its competitors.

Publicly Sovereign's directors displayed a sense of pride that they had finally succeeded in getting the cab off the rank. Chairman Bruce Bornholdt spoke for all of them when he said, "This has been a landmark year for Sovereign culminating with its successful listing on the New Zealand Stock Exchange, and I am proud to have been Sovereign's chairman at such an important stage in its history. Listing has been a Sovereign objective for a number of years, and this will provide the capital which will be needed to support Sovereign's future growth." Ironically it was to be his last public statement as chairman.

Sovereign's share price languished because there was no interest from the local investment houses, which were its competitors of course. The share price rose directly after the listing and then dropped to a low of $1.40. Eventually it rose again to hover around its original listing price of $2.25 per share. Thus, despite all the work that went into the listing Sovereign still needed more capital in order to grow. Coon's worst fears had been realised in that Sovereign was caught in a no-man's land between being a company that was too big to be small, and one that was too small to be big. Sovereign needed to grow rapidly, at a rate that could only be achieved by acquisition, as had been accomplished with the purchase of MetLife. There was some urgency to do this because the New Zealand life industry continued to be characterised by strategic affiliations and buyouts. Colonial had increased its muscle by purchasing Prudential, and Sun Alliance had purchased both Norwich Union and Guardian. Sun Alliance's purchase of Norwich was a particularly heavy blow to Sovereign because Coon and Hendry had hoped to purchase it themselves. The English owners had made it very clear, however, that they had no interest in selling to Sovereign. Coon, and especially Hendry, took the snub personally. It was another in the string of disappointments.

Coon and Hendry were stymied. There were no more small companies in New Zealand they could realistically consider acquiring. Moreover, the New Zealand economy had gone off the boil and the chances of raising capital locally were slim. Press reports quoted Sovereign non-executive directors as saying, "under the present share holding situation, Sovereign was likely to need additional capital. In the current economic environment, raising capital to fund acquisitions is more difficult." Richard Coon made some attempts to secure funding from overseas investors but most said they were not interested because of the small size of the New Zealand economy. At times, the future looked bleak.

In the end, Sovereign was saved by a white knight in the guise of a robot.

CHAPTER 19
A new beginning

"We are buying something that has a very successful formula so it would be pretty arrogant of us to come and say we have another formula that will work better. What we want to do is to build on what is a very good platform and capture the benefits that we have identified with regard to products and process."

In December of 1998, ten years from the time Coon and Hendry were sitting in their little office in Takapuna on borrowed furniture with a few key staff scrambling to get ready to open for business in January of 1989, Sovereign became an autonomous 100% owned subsidiary of ASB Bank. The company was de-listed from the New Zealand stock exchange after being listed for only eight months.

The ASB Bank purchase resulted from a chance meeting between David Belcher of Clavell, who has been involved in every one of Sovereign's major financial transactions, and Ralph Norris, managing director of the ASB. Both are old boys of Lynfield College and had recently joined an old pupils' foundation. At the end of one of the foundation's meetings, Belcher told Norris he would like to have a chat with him. When they met, Belcher suggested that ASB Bank might like to consider buying Sovereign. Belcher said that Sovereign was looking for an association that could take the company further and that he believed the ASB culture was consistent with Sovereign's. "I was interested," says Norris, "because we had been looking to acquire another company. We were looking to broaden our base so the timing was fortuitous. I knew nothing negative about Sovereign. In fact, I knew very little about them at all except they were an insurance company going somewhere quickly." Of course, Sovereign was not a completely unknown commodity to ASB. It had been Sovereign's bankers for eight years and, at one time, had been the company's landlord. Moreover, Norris was working for Ferrier when Ferrier was asked to chair Sovereign. "I knew that Dennis had done his own rigorous analysis," says Norris, "and that, if there had been any problems with Sovereign, he would have resigned his position as he did at the Housing Corporation."

Norris met with Coon and Hendry and was impressed. "Ian struck me as being aggressive in a very positive sense. He knew what he wanted and he was a straight shooter. He was clearly proud of what he and Chris had accomplished. Chris impressed me as being a great thinker," he adds. "He was not the stereotypical actuary. He could think outside the square. I was also impressed that both Chris and Ian had a very strong commitment to their staff and to their culture." Norris continued to explore the idea of purchasing Sovereign, and the more he learned about the company, the more convinced he became that it would be great for both parties. "We saw Sovereign as a very innovative company with good technology and the same strong focus on its customers as we have at ASB," he says. Certainly both companies shared a commitment to customer service and both had won the respect of its customers. Sovereign was typically judged by advisers as the company they most preferred to deal with, and ASB Bank consistently has the highest customer satisfaction ratings of any bank in New Zealand. Both companies had also earned the reputation of being committed to looking after their staff and to supporting the community. It seemed like the perfect match.

> *"Sovereign is a good fit for ASB and it gives the bank a platform to become a broader based financial services company."*

ASB Bank offered $235 million for Sovereign, a price that was considered reasonable in an independent appraisal prepared by Grant Samuel and Associates. The offer was accepted by Coon and Hendry, and the rest of the Sovereign board, and they recommended to other shareholders they accept the offer, too.

From the bank's point of view, the purchase of Sovereign was not a rescue bid but rather allowed the ASB to expand from being simply a trading bank. "Sovereign is a good fit for ASB and it gives the bank a platform to become a broader based financial services company," says Norris. Just as Sovereign had been with the MetLife merger, the ASB was very careful about how they approached the Sovereign takeover. "In the case of 80% of mergers a lot of value is lost through an aggressive direct integration approach and the winners are usually only the shareholders of the target company," says Norris. "With

Sovereign, the ASB took a conservative gentle approach. We wanted to run Sovereign autonomously, and certainly didn't want to jam it together as per the standard bank-assurance model." Norris was astute enough to know he had bought a company that had a very successful formula. "It would have been pretty arrogant of us to come and say we have another formula that will work better," he says. "What we wanted to do was build on what was a very good platform and capture the benefits that we identified with regard to products and process."

The New Zealand news media saw the ASB acquisition of Sovereign as one of the most intriguing plays in the financial services industry. "The move is curious because it is a bank taking over an insurance company," wrote the New Zealand Herald. "Up until this transaction the merger and acquisition game was being played by like-minded companies. That is, insurance companies buying insurance companies." It would soon become clear that this was the beginning of a complete integration of the banking and insurance industries. By 2000, the Commonwealth Bank of Australia, the major shareholder of ASB Bank, was making a bid for Colonial which operated a financial services business in New Zealand and Australia, and which had itself over the years acquired two other insurance companies, Prudential and NZI.

Coon received $46 million from the sale, Hendry $15 million, and other original shareholders, such as Uganecz, received substantial payouts. Board members such as Belcher, who collected his listing fee, and chairman Bruce Bornholdt, also benefited handsomely. Ironically, both Belcher and Bornholdt were casualties of the sale, as were other non-executive directors. One of Hendry's first tasks after the purchase was to tell Bornholdt that his chairmanship was terminated. This was difficult for Hendry because the two had become personal friends. They had been through a lot together since the first battle with the Securities Commission. Bornholdt reacted badly to the news. He had let his legal practice slide over the years as he poured more and more time and energy into Sovereign. This made it worse for Hendry, as loyalty is a very important part of his character. He hoped that at least the cash Bornholdt had in hand would be some compensation. In the end, it didn't matter. Within 18 months, Bornholdt had died of cancer. Not everyone benefited financially from the ASB buy-out. Those who lost out were the small shareholders who received only what they had originally paid for the shares at the time of listing. The independent advisers who had participated in the broker share option scheme called the Partnership Spirit, also missed out on the full potential of the scheme. For them to have received any substantial payout, the shares needed to have been listed and traded over a number of years.

After the sale, it was expected that it would continue to be business as usual at Sovereign. The purchase agreement called for key management to remain, and Hendry and Coon negotiated an involvement to the end of 2001. Hendry agreed to remain group managing director, the job he never wanted in the first place, and so prior to Christmas of 1998, he was apprehensive about how this arrangement would work out. He was concerned about what it would be like to have someone over him as boss after ten years of calling the shots. He also wondered about how the chemistry would work between himself and Norris, who replaced Bornholdt as chairman of Sovereign. But by early 1999, his concerns seemed unfounded. "They have been very good owners," he said at the time. "They have allowed us to operate independently. They have not interfered with our strategy or in the day-to-day management of the company, and, they have seen the benefit as a result." Norris initially took a low-key approach to owning Sovereign. Perhaps because ASB Bank is controlled by the Commonwealth Bank of Australia, Norris understood what it was like to operate a company which is owned by another. "Ralph understood the difference between the role of chairman and managing director," says Hendry. "He has enough sense to know the bank doesn't know how to run a life insurance company."

The change in ownership resulted in improvements to the way Sovereign operated at the senior management level. "There was a founder's mentality in Sovereign," says Norris. "Coon and Hendry felt they could make decisions on their own based on an analysis that sometimes lacked rigour. Since taking over, we have worked hard to put in place systems that are world-best practices, particularly in the area of financial reporting." Hendry agrees. "They helped us to become more disciplined in our financial reporting," he says. "They introduced us to their style and format of reporting to the board, and this has enhanced the quality of the information we provide." The improvements in reporting have actually worked to Sovereign's advantage because, according to Hendry, "the more information we gave them, the more confidence they had in the way Sovereign operated." Perhaps as a result of these improvements, board meetings under Norris became shorter and more like the meetings of a management committee. Freed from the requirements and complexities of being a public company, and without the need to focus on raising capital, meetings were more matter-of-fact and focused mostly on the numbers. They also became more serious without Bornholdt's extremely clever wit. Nevertheless, a very warm relationship developed between Sovereign people and the senior ASB managers they dealt with.

The new Sovereign board did make some immediate changes to the company's holdings. S H Lock was transferred into ASB Bank because "its business activity fitted better with a bank than with a life insurance company," says Norris. Reeves Moses was sold as it was deemed to detract from Sovereign's core business. Caledonian was run more as a department of Sovereign than as an independent company, a trend that had been developing over the past two years. Caledonian was later scrapped completely and its advisers became part of the Sovereign Network. It was also agreed that the sale of Successful Money Management Seminars back to Laura and Okke Hansen would proceed in April of 2000 as Coon and Hendry had planned.

The ASB Bank purchase of Sovereign provided the company that had revolutionised the life industry in New Zealand with the opportunity for a new beginning. Free from the pressures of raising capital and going through a public listing, and with the support of one of New Zealand's most successful banks, Coon and Hendry were able to focus once again on what they did best, building a successful financial services company. With the sale behind them, the two men who came to New Zealand with a dream of starting a life insurance company were determined that Sovereign would raise its performance to yet another level and end the millennium on a high.

And they succeeded.

CHAPTER 20

We're back

"Let me make it clear that Chris, Richard and I are back. We are re-energised and completely focused on the task of leading the company into the next millennium."

Sovereign began its second decade of being in business with some significant fence mending and damage control to be done, particularly among the broker network. Sovereign's competition, in particular David Whyte, Sovereign's first broker development manager and now head of rival life company, AIA, were making mischief by saying that the big bad wolf, ASB bank, would be coming to their door to take all their clients away. Many staff were unsettled, too, because they were apprehensive about what life would be like working for a large corporate. On the other hand, after years of distractions and disappointments around the stock market listing, the abandoned foray in Australia and the New Zealand Superannuation Service fiasco, there was a sense of relief and excitement about a new direction. "We swapped the sleepless nights of cold sweat for the daily level of frustration that was tolerable," says Coon dryly. To many staff, it was almost as if Sovereign was being reborn. Tired of being kicked around by the competition, many were saying quite confidently, "we're back!" There was a feeling of achievement among Sovereign's staff, too. They were proud that the company that had started in a pokey office with borrowed furniture, ten years later had an annual premium income of $100 million, $500 million in funds under management, $800 million in its mortgage book and over 200,000 clients. Its sale price of $235 million was a tangible measure of the success that had been achieved.

On his return from golfing in Bali, Hendry was energised, focused and committed. Around the time of the buyout, he had been reluctant to take the limelight away from the ASB Bank, but on his return he gathered Sovereign's staff together. It was the closest he had ever come to a fireside chat, and it was the most open and eloquent he had ever been in a public gathering. Honest and emotional, but with a sense of a weight lifted from his shoulders, he reviewed Sovereign's history and outlined the way ahead. "As I considered what I would say to you," he began, "I was struck by the fact many of you are relatively new to us. Unlike Naomi (Ballantyne) and Russell (Hutchinson) who have been with us from the beginning, you don't know our history. To many of you, Sovereign was a large, well-established and successful company when you joined. You weren't around:

- when Sovereign was a dream in an attic (August 1988);
- when no-one rang (January 1989);
- during the dark days with the Securities Commission (1990);
- when we saw the demise of HomePlan (1990);
- when Eagle Star attempted to steal our business.

"There were many other character building moments as we have made bad decisions or put our faith in the wrong people. But equally, there have been wonderful times:

- the thrill of watching those early proposals come in;
- our move to Hurstmere Road;
- the first Taylor Survey which put us first;
- the growth of our people and their pride in Sovereign;
- the high standards we set and achieved in service performance;
- Sovereign's Christmas Party traditions;
- recognition of Sovereign as New Zealand's leading life insurance company.

"All of us know from our own personal lives that we have to be able to take the rough with the smooth, and life at Sovereign has been no different. The harder we tried, the more mistakes we made. And, Sovereign has made plenty:

- choosing to work with brokers who turned out to be poor or dishonest;
- developing systems that didn't work well such as Quicksmart;
- occasionally hiring the wrong people;
- some unsuccessful initiatives such as entering Australia in 1994 and NZSS.

"But we're still here so we must have done some things right. In fact, it's my philosophy that I would rather make a decision quickly, which may prove to be wrong, than be frightened to make a decision in case I make a mistake. We must never lose our entrepreneurial spirit, but we must put in place guidelines which will protect us from our worst excesses. Having said that, Sovereign will always be about taking calculated risks. After all, Chris and I started by taking a huge risk 10 years ago.

"I will always be in Chris's debt for providing me with the opportunity to share in the Sovereign adventure. It's been an exhilarating experience and we are passing on a powerful legacy. Because Sovereign is no longer Chris and I. Today, it's bigger and more important than we are, and it needs the combined talents and energy of the people in this room to take it to the next stage of its successful development.

"Chris, Richard and I have been criticised, with every justification, for being so involved with the stock market listing that we have not devoted enough time to running the business. This is absolutely true. But during this period of neglect, we have achieved some of our finest results:

- the launch of Aegis;
- the development of Unit Trusts;
- entering the mortgage business;
- introducing the share options scheme;
- the development of Platform Z;
- opening the Sovereign Call Centre;
- growing our market share.

"How did we do that? I think it's because each of you recognise you are a member of a high performing family, and because you take personal responsibility for making sure your job gets done. And we are going to give you much more opportunity to demonstrate that quality in the future by including you much more directly in the decision making process.

With a revitalised and refocused Hendry at the helm, the company's performance broke all previous records.

But before I get to that, let me make it clear that Chris, Richard and I are back. We are energised and completely focused on the task of leading the company into the next millennium."

On that note Sovereign began its second decade of being in business. With a revitalised and refocused Hendry at the helm, the company's performance broke all previous records. "Many people saw the ASB purchase as being the end of Sovereign," says Hendry, "but we have been more dynamic and successful since." Hendry gives much of the credit for Sovereign's stellar performance to David Haak, who had joined Sovereign in 1994 and who had taken over as director of distribution after David Anderson resigned in late 1999. "Ian took a risk in putting me in," says Haak modestly, "and then letting me go to it. We had a good team and sales were good. But in some ways the company was dysfunctional because of the conflict that had existed between Ballantyne and Anderson." One of Haak's first challenges was to improve the relationship between distribution, operations and marketing. "That was a priority," he says, "because if one is out of sync, none of it will work effectively."

The second challenge that Haak faced was that the independent advisers supporting Sovereign had not reacted well to the ASB purchase. They believed the bank would use its own people to cross market Sovereign's products and, therefore, be in competition with them. Haak was not only able to reassure them that this was not likely to happen because bank staff did not understand the Sovereign products, but he demonstrated that more than ever Sovereign was committed to making them successful. "We drove a different focus on how we dealt with the advisers," says Haak. Our focus was not on service levels or rates of commission, but on developing a business relationship with them." The first step was to remove the silos that existed within distribution and to integrate the sales teams into one unit so that everyone could sell every type of product. "This was a bold move," says Haak, "because some people did not have the skills they should have had. The reorganisation caused stress for people," he admits. The second step was to give the business development managers (BDMs) who worked with the independent advisers, a reason to call on them. Resource kits were developed showing advisers how they could improve a certain area of their business. One might be on advertising, for example, another on selling skills and a third on office systems. "With these kits, the BDMs could easily drop in and meet with the advisers as experts on business management" says Haak, "and talk to them about how they could improve their own businesses. We gave the advisers a reason to associate with Sovereign and the tools they would need to sell Sovereign products." It was well received by the advisers and Sovereign grew its regular producing force from 400 to 550 as a result. "Because everyone worked together, it was so easy to do," says Haak.

Overall Sovereign had a relationship with 1500 independent advisers, although only one-third were regular producers. "The challenge," says Haak, "was to convert more advisers into regular producers. The problem was that BDMs liked to stay in their comfort zones and spend their time talking to advisers who were already supporting Sovereign, instead of talking to those who did not." Haak wanted BDMs to spend only 20% of their face-to-face contact time with the regular producers and the rest with the other advisers. But because BDMs spend a lot of time travelling, they have a great deal of time to talk on the telephones. Haak believed that if the BDMs spent 60% of their telephone time talking to the regular producers, they could maintain those key relationships. To make this new approach work, Sovereign has invested a great deal of money in developing specialists within the distribution team who can support the BDMs by working directly with advisers who have particular needs. Haak's strategy was very effective. "We had a well-oiled machine," he says. "One year after the ASB purchase we were achieving growth of just on 40% per year, and we had 22% of the market."

Two years later, many staff who have been at Sovereign a long time can see the company changing as a result of the ASB purchase. Some see the changes as being relatively minor. "There have not been huge frustrations for me, personally," says Coon, "although everything takes a lot longer to do now, for example to make decisions about funding and tax matters. It used to take 1-2 months for us to develop new products but now it can take 14 months." Other staff also talk about how much longer it now takes to get things done because control for some of Sovereign's internal administration lies with ASB Bank's departmental managers. They speak of internal politics affecting the quality of decisions, about people being afraid to speak out when issues are being discussed and decisions are being made, and about things being slowed down by bureaucracy. The Sovereign style was to do things. Need to fit out an office? Go and buy the furniture to do it. Something not working in the building? Get a contractor to fix it. The bank's style on the other hand, is described as being one of control: submit a form, wait (and wait) while the request is processed, and end up with an inferior quality job done at a more expensive price as a result. But, on balance, most Sovereign employees agree that the ASB Bank purchase has had little significant effect on the day-to-day running of the company.

In any event, the impact of ASB purchase of Sovereign was quickly overshadowed by a much more dramatic event.

CHAPTER 21

The Colonial merger: another great leap forward

"This surprised me. I expected CBA would want to run life assurance from Australia underneath Colonial."

No sooner had Hendry re-focused and re-energised the people at Sovereign after the short-lived public listing and the ASB purchase, no sooner had the staff adjusted to the new corporate ways of doing business that had slowly crept into their lives, than the apple cart was well and truly tipped upside down yet again.

The new challenge for Sovereign's management and staff was the merger of Colonial, one of New Zealand's oldest and largest life companies, into the Sovereign Group. ASB Bank's parent, the Commonwealth Bank of Australia (CBA), had successfully purchased Colonial in Australia in 2000 as part of its strategy of becoming an integrated financial services company. It was not a straightforward process. First agreement had to be reached about the price, then the regulatory authorities in each country had to approve the sale, and then changes had to be made to ASB Bank's ownership, freeing it from the constraint of being 25% owned by a community trust. Once those obstacles were out of the way, CBA and ASB had to make a tough decision. They had to decide what to do with the two life insurance companies it now owned in New Zealand. The options were to allow Sovereign and Colonial to continue to operate independently, or to merge one into the other. The first option was never given serious consideration because it would result in too much duplication of activity and cost. The second was the option that made the most sense, to merge one company into the other, thereby achieving economies of scale and one single brand.

Having decided to merge one company into the other, the problem was which way to go. Should Colonial, the well-established New Zealand company with a well known brand in both New Zealand and Australia take over the young upstart, or should the dynamic new kid on the block with a track record of recent phenomenal success take over the ageing giant? In the end, the decision was made to make Colonial part of Sovereign. "This surprised me," says Coon. "I expected CBA would want to run life assurance from Australia underneath Colonial." But Sovereign was a much better managed company with newer technology and more powerful systems. More importantly, although it was not as well known as Colonial in the marketplace generally, the Sovereign brand was well known and better liked in the market that mattered most, that of the independent adviser.

"The merger was a big shock because you had two opposites coming together."

Assimilating Colonial into Sovereign was a huge challenge, much bigger than when Sovereign took over MetLife. A total of between 60 and 70 Colonial staff moved from Wellington to Auckland, and there were approximately another 200 Colonial staff who remained in Wellington to run the office, now re-branded as Sovereign. The merger with Colonial was also to have a bigger impact on Sovereign than even the ASB Bank purchase. "The major change at Sovereign was the Colonial merger," says Errol Timmins. "This was very different from the MetLife merger because it was an arranged marriage. Also, Colonial was a much larger organisation and, therefore, not so easy to assimilate." Haak agrees. "The merger was a big shock," he says, "because you had two opposites coming together." Ballantyne was of the opinion there was a huge downside to the merger. "I always saw the forced merger between Sovereign and Colonial as being a lose-lose for everyone," she says. "I never believed the synergies would be there like they were with MetLife."

One reason this merger was more difficult than the MetLife merger was that Sovereign now had its ASB masters to contend with, and their views on how to integrate the two companies were not the same as Sovereign's. "The bank had never gone through a merger," says Ballantyne who had had the primary responsibility for merging MetLife into Sovereign a few years earlier. "They started to become involved and make decisions that were good for the bank, or for them personally, but which could have seriously hurt Sovereign." According to Ballantyne, the bank set the rules for how the merger would take place, and they did not seem interested in hearing from Sovereign staff. "We had absolutely no say in anything," says Ballantyne. "A consulting firm was brought in to tell us how to do it, which was a real slap in the face given that we had had a successful

MetLife merger. In fact," she adds, "we were told never to mention MetLife." In the field, it was even worse. "I was sent to Wellington to take the lead on the merger," says Ballantyne, "but I didn't really have the lead role. I was to take over from the CEO but his direct reports had not been told. I had no support at all."

After the people issue, the major hurdle to bringing the companies together was their operating systems. Again, the task was more complicated than it had been in the MetLife merger. "We had two systems," says Coon, "ours and MetLife's, and Colonial had a mixture of many systems from previous mergers." Timmins agrees that the operational side of the merger has been even more difficult than the people side. "Colonial had a larger in-force client base because of its age. It has also been harder to do things because of legacy issues related to IT. Sovereign didn't understand how difficult it would be because Colonial is not one company but is really 16 companies as a result of the acquisitions Colonial has made in recent times that were never bedded down properly.

Not surprisingly, the merger did not go smoothly. Not only were there problems in the management of the project, there were fundamental challenges in the merging of the companies themselves. Whereas MetLife and Sovereign had similar cultures, Colonial's was that of a traditional life assurance company. This gulf affected how people saw each other. "There was a high level of distrust on both sides," says Coon. Timmins agrees that the differences between the cultures of the two organisations has been an issue. "It has not been easy," he says. 'The process of compromise hasn't been smooth. On a personal level," he adds, "one of my biggest challenges has been to counter the fear and suspicion Colonial employees held towards Sovereign. I was surprised at the level of resistance we have encountered in operations. It has lasted a long time, I suppose because traditionally they have seen us as the enemy." One of the main problems was that the Colonial people were not inducted into the Sovereign culture very well. Indeed, it seemed like there was some doubt in people's minds about who was merging with whom. There were conflicting viewpoints on which culture should be dominant. At first, Hendry told everyone there would be a new culture that combined elements of both organisations but this just added to the confusion. "Later, Ian made clear the core values he wanted in the new culture," says Timmins. "After that most former Colonial people adjusted to the Sovereign culture," he explains. Not all ex-Colonial staff made the adjustment, however. Many stuck together in cliques and this made it harder to integrate them into the Sovereign culture.

The culture differences also affected how senior managers thought the company should be run. "There were senior people from Colonial who were put in key positions," says Ballantyne, "and they kept saying things that were the opposite of what we had always held to be important at Sovereign. For example, they were suggesting we abandon the two-day standard for turning around new applications and go to a seven-day turnaround period to save money. It was always about cost-cutting, never about providing good service." Sovereign management also encountered some situations they had never encountered before. There was a high level of union membership among Colonial staff, for example, and Sovereign management had to deal with this issue for the first time.

> *The integration of Colonial into Sovereign was not helped by the resignation of Naomi Ballantyne.*

The integration of Colonial into Sovereign was not helped by the resignation of Naomi Ballantyne in October of 2000. This was not a happy parting. For ten years, Ballantyne had enjoyed the complete confidence of Coon and Hendry. Over the years, she had been given challenge after challenge to handle, and she had always performed well, to the point that she was known as Sovereign's trouble-shooter. Shortly after the ASB Bank purchase, Ballantyne was appointed Sovereign's Chief Operating Officer and it looked to everyone as if she was being groomed to be Hendry's successor. Unfortunately, Sovereign's masters at ASB did not share Coon and Hendry's view of Ballantyne's ability, and Ballantyne started to get that message. "It was made very clear to me that I was not going to be Ian's successor," she says, "but I don't think they expected I would leave. Otherwise they would have put a restraint in trade in place preventing me from starting up in opposition to them. They didn't and I think they feel silly about that now."

The conflict between Ballantyne and ASB's management was most likely the result of what happens when corporate culture meets entrepreneurial spirit. From the time she joined Sovereign, Ballantyne has always made it very clear that she has no time for the corporate way of doing business. She is intolerant of office politics, contemptuous of the corporate obsession with internal issues and impatient with bureaucracy. She is also not one to keep these views to herself. "I just couldn't stomach it any more," she says with characteristic bluntness when asked why she left Sovereign. Nevertheless, the decision was not an easy one for Ballantyne. She is very loyal to both Coon and Hendry. In the event, the straw that broke the camel's back came while Hendry was overseas. "Ian's absence made it much easier to resign," she says, "although I felt badly that I was doing it while he was away." Both Coon and Hendry wish the outcome had been different. "It is sad that she left," says Coon. "She did not believe that she was getting the respect that was due to her, and she ended up in conflict with some of the ASB people."

To make matters even worse, in the eyes of ASB in any case, Ballantyne decided to set up a new life company in competition with Sovereign. Because independent advisers like to have more than one company's products to recommend to their clients, neither Ballantyne nor the people at Sovereign saw much problem with this. Coon even thinks they should have supported her financially. "That way we would have had some control," he says. "I thought she could potentially do a lot of damage to Sovereign, and make it more difficult for us to introduce the new products I want to introduce into the market." ASB Bank did not see it that way. Norris, in particular, took it as a personal affront that she would open in opposition to Sovereign.

Understandably, Ballantyne's departure had a marked affect on Sovereign staff. "I was in Wellington the day Naomi resigned," says Gruebner. "The curtain came down on my world because I knew that things would be different and that has proved to be the case. That devastating day made me depressed, and I looked at where I would go from here." It was the same for other long-time employees, such as Errol Timmins. "Naomi's departure sent ripples throughout the place," he says. "There was shock and disbelief. People kept asking questions to try to understand it. Her resignation created doubts and concerns for quite a while," he says. " Most people wish her well on a personal level but it is a hell of a challenge for us." Today Timmins, Gruebner and others have come to grips with her resignation but she is clearly missed. It is almost impossible to talk to any long-standing Sovereign employee about the company without them talking positively about Ballantyne and what she did. "I have personally found it very unsettling," says Timmins.

In truth, Naomi was not the only person to have reservations about the Sovereign merger with Colonial. Hendry and Coon expressed the view at the outset that Colonial's New Zealand life operation should be sold out of the group rather than merged with Sovereign. In their view, the two companies were a very poor fit, and Sovereign would be damaged by the integration. "Sovereign was a progressive, modern, efficient, growth-oriented company with a powerful inclusive corporate culture," says Hendry. "Colonial, by contrast, was an old traditional life office with massive legacy system problems and inefficiencies. It had a cost-cutting mentality and very little interest in staff empowerment. And it was in Wellington."

When Hendry and Coon's view was rejected, Hendry set out to make the integration as successful as possible despite his reservations. Forty-four work-stream groups were established to consider every aspect of the integration process. "Staff from both companies participated constructively in these groups," says Hendry, "and they produced some excellent plans." In spite of this planning, the problems of what to do about the legacy systems, and how to cope with the reluctance of most Colonial staff to move from Wellington were very difficult to resolve. In fact the legacy systems will haunt Sovereign for some years to come.

"These are just temporary challenges which will be overcome."

Hendry knew from his experience with the MetLife merger that the way staff were treated during the integration would be a critical factor in the success of the exercise. Although one of the objectives was to reduce the combined staff numbers from approximately 1050 to under 800, he hoped that attrition, through voluntary redundancies and resignations, would keep the compulsory redundancies to a minimum. For the most part, this is what happened, and today Sovereign's staff numbers around 800.

Hendry's fears about the damage integration would cause to Sovereign's service standards and operating efficiencies proved to be only too accurate, and he freely admits that the initial impacts were difficult to manage. Nevertheless he is confident that Sovereign will recover. "The short-term effects were negative," he says, "but the longer term benefits and opportunities far outweigh those early problems. We will re-establish our reputation. This is not a new situation for us. It existed after the MetLife acquisition. These are just temporary challenges which will be overcome."

Indeed, Hendry can already see that the new Sovereign has gained some significant benefits from the integration with Colonial. One of these, for instance, is that the addition of many high calibre Colonial staff has strengthened Sovereign's talent pool. Another is that Sovereign now has an enhanced product range, particularly in the savings and investment areas. The integration has also given Sovereign a broader distribution network through which it can promote products such as Sovereign Home Loans. Timmins agrees that the integration is already paying dividends. "We can already see the big advantages merging the two companies has given us. We have more resources now and there shouldn't be anything that we cannot do."

By the end of 2000, after the biggest phase of the integration had been completed, Hendry was as positive about Sovereign's future as he was when he and Coon launched the company in 1989. "If prior to the integration there was ever any doubt about Sovereign's long-term future, this has totally disappeared," he said at the time. "Sovereign remains the clear market leader amongst New Zealand life offices, and I believe this company will continue to influence the development of the market."

While in a perfect world there would have been a period of consolidation after the integration, that is not how things usually work in Sovereign's world.

Another thunderbolt was about to arrive.

CHAPTER 22
The challenge ahead

"I would much rather be in Sovereign than in any other insurance company in town."

After going through the ASB Bank purchase, the Colonial merger and Ballantyne's departure, most Sovereign employees had taken comfort from the knowledge that Hendry was still running the company. But in the winter of 2001, their worst nightmares came true as Hendry decided it was time to leave. "As the organisation gets bigger, you have to let go," says Hendry. "When you do, people will make different decisions from the ones you would have made, but you have to let them do it." It is not always easy to sit back and watch that happen, and that is perhaps why Hendry plans a short break from New Zealand. "I am going on a 53 night cruise and then I'm open to offers," he laughs. Those who know Hendry well know the reality is likely to be different. He will perfect his golf and enjoy his family, but how long before he is involved with business again? That is the question. "Anyway," continues Hendry, "New Zealand will shut down over Christmas and I've given up trying to hold the annual sales conference in January. None of the arguments I've ever put forward have persuaded anybody," he says with a smile, referring to the long-standing company joke that every year he would try to get independent advisers back on the job right after New Year's. He never did.

A few weeks after Hendry made his decision, Coon decided that it was time for him to move on too, although he is not ready to completely let go. "Some of the excitement has gone. It is no longer the business it was," he says. "It is not as challenging. You do not need to be so clever." So, why is he still holding on by coming back part-time as a consultant? "I am delighted to accept a consultancy," says Coon, "because I have a deep respect for the ASB Bank, and because I am only too happy to provide any help I can to ensure Sovereign remains a first-rate company." Coon will also do some consulting overseas for the reassurers he has known over the years." I also have some other actuarial ideas I want to work on," he adds.

As always, boating will also be very important to him.

Since Uganecz had resigned in 1999 after the ASB purchase, the resignations of Ballantyne, Hendry and Coon means that Sovereign will enter 2002, its 13th year of operation, without any of the company's founding managers actively leading the company. To minimise the disruption this would cause, and in an attempt to provide some continuity as the company went forward to an uncertain future, Hendry advocated that his replacement come from within the organisation. Norris, Sovereign's chairman, did not agree and opted instead to appoint an outsider. In fairness to Norris, he did not believe he had many choices. Ballantyne had gone, Haak was relatively new in his role as Director of Distribution and had not had a lot of experience in financial management, and Richard Coon, on the other hand, had expertise in financial management but little experience in people management or with sales. Hendry had recommended that David Haak and Richard Coon be appointed joint managing directors. "This looked like a good solution to me," he says. "Each complimented the other, they had worked together over the last couple of years, and they were both steeped in the Sovereign culture. Chris and I had been joint managing directors in the beginning," he adds. "That arrangement had worked for us, and I believed it would work for Richard and David." Perhaps because, unlike Hendry, he had never experienced working in a partnership, Norris did not agree. "I think Ralph felt that not being able to choose one person for the role was a sign of weakness," says Hendry.

The challenge ahead will be to keep the Sovereign culture intact, and maintain the relationships Sovereign has developed over the years with independent advisers.

In September of 2001, the Sovereign board named Simon Swanson, who is currently managing director of Colonial Fiji Limited, as managing director of the Sovereign Group. The challenge for Swanson, who takes the reins from Hendry January 1, 2002, and Hugh Burrett, the new managing director of ASB Bank who succeeded Norris as chairman of the Sovereign Group in October of 2001, will be to keep the Sovereign culture intact, and maintain the relationships Sovereign has developed over the years with independent advisers. Coon and Hendry are both confident that the Sovereign culture will continue to flourish. Chris Coon will still be associated with the company as a consultant, and his brother Richard will remain on the senior management team. In Hendry's eyes, David Haak will be a key person in keeping the Sovereign culture alive. "In David, Sovereign has a person who epitomises all the Sovereign values," he says, "and he has the passion to drive Sovereign forward." Haak and Richard Coon will also have the support of long-standing employees such as Errol Timmins, Lyn Dorreen, Ted Gruebner, Paul Bravo, Angela Eastwood, Ian Pe rry and many others too numerous to mention.

On the verge of their retirement, both Coon and Hendry look back with satisfaction at what they have achieved. As they have always done, they acknowledge each other's contribution to the company's success. "Chris was the architect," says Hendry. "Sovereign is his creation." In a separate interview, Coon is quick to praise Hendry. "I couldn't have done this without Ian," he says. "Our relationship has been a major ingredient in our success. We have an understanding that is incredibly rare. Although we are totally different people, I often know the words he is going to use at the end of a sentence, and when we are out we often order the same things."

They also agree that the experience of building Sovereign has been a wonderful one. "It has been a great run for both of us," says Hendry. " I have absolutely no regrets." It is the same for Coon. "It has been a hugely satisfying ride," he says, "both because of the professional challenge and because of the friendships we have developed." Have they had to pay a high price for that experience? "Not at all," says Coon. "We have had an almost charmed existence." As usual, they see it the same way. "No, the price has not been too high," says Hendry. "Of course, it has not been a 9 to 5 job. All of your waking hours have been devoted to Sovereign and so you have had to be really committed. Clearly all the family has had to be committed, too, and give you support. I am lucky that mine has been."

One of the questions waiting to be answered is whether the principles behind the Sovereign way of doing business, which have been the main ingredients in the company's success to date, will continue to drive Sovereign forward, or whether they will slowly disappear as traditional corporate behaviours create a new Sovereign that is essentially no different from its long-time competitors. The other question is whether the much larger organisation with its corporate management structure can respond to the marketplace quickly enough. After all, it is much harder for a large organisation to respond quickly to new opportunities or its customers' needs. There are simply more stakeholders. It takes longer to get decisions made and to get everyone's buy-in. "The 'do it now' way of thinking and behaving has become more difficult," says Timmins. "Sovereign's family orientation is still there but it is not as strong as it was. It is far harder to keep that feeling when you have a large number of people in different locations with different histories."

Today, nearly 13 years after it first opened its doors for business, Sovereign is again a dynamic, progressive and highly successful company, and it enters its next phase with a solid foundation on which to build. Sovereign may no longer be a small company but at least it is still locally owned and controlled. Whereas most of its competitors have to go offshore to get major decisions made, Sovereign's senior executives and directors are close at hand. The company is still a great employer. Sovereign's gymnasium is twice the size it was, and staff have access to well-being lectures and health checks. Over 30 company sports teams receive uniforms and other forms of sponsorship. Members of the Dragon Boat team are paid up to $30,000 per year to travel around New Zealand to compete in events, for example. It is true that the company stopped giving each employee a Christmas hamper when the company grew to more than 100 employees; however, everyone still gets an Easter egg. There is a formal black tie Christmas party and a spectacular mid-year function for all staff and their partners. In addition, there is an annual Christmas party for children. None of these may seem significant by themselves, but together they are a constant reminder to staff that Sovereign values them. "We spend 50 times more money on staff benefits today," says Hendry, "than we did in the early days."

Even more importantly, in what is universally acknowledged to be a tough market for financial services companies, Sovereign is a strong business. In fact, it is really four strong businesses. In its core business of life insurance, it is the largest writer of new business and has by far the largest market share of any life company in New Zealand. As an investment company, it is one of the top five in New Zealand with $3.5 billion in funds under management. Sovereign is one of New Zealand's major fund managers. Aegis, which Sovereign built from the ground up, is the most successful wrap account in the country and administers $2 billion of investors' funds. Sovereign is also a major player in the home lending business. It is the largest non-bank lender of mortgage funds and has a mortgage book of

$1.75 billion. In short, Sovereign is a solid broadly based financial service company with a diversified range of products and services. "Sovereign is the market leader, or close to it, in each of its core business areas," says Hendry with pride. "And the company is well positioned for future growth in each of these areas."

Only time will tell whether Sovereign will continue to be the market innovator and trendsetter, but Hendry is very confident that it will be. "This is a difficult market for all insurance companies," he says, "and Sovereign is in a much better position to go forward than most of its competitors." He may be right. National Mutual, now owned by AXA was on the ropes not long ago, and rumours in the marketplace suggest Tower is struggling at the moment. AMP seems to have lost its way and Royal & SunAlliance is trying to sell off its life business worldwide. "I would much rather be in Sovereign than in any other insurance company in town," Hendry states emphatically.

"Sovereign is the market leader, or close to it, in each of its core business areas, and the company is well positioned for future growth in each of these areas."

No matter what happens in the future, nothing can diminish the story of Sovereign's amazing growth, from being an idea that nearly everyone thought was crazy, to becoming a company, which began its life operating with virtually no money, and ended up being one of New Zealand's most successful companies with market share twice as big as its nearest competitor in the life industry.

At the very least, Chris Coon and Ian Hendry have reminded the rest of us of what can be done with a dream, determination and hard work.

EPILOGUE
What you can learn from the Sovereign story

"We often discover that people we view as overnight successes have in fact laboured for years in obscurity before they were finally recognised and rewarded for their contributions. Success is a cumulative effort; the journey to the top in any field is usually long and requires careful planning."
Dr Napoleon Hill

The story of Sovereign Assurance is much more than just an interesting business story or inspirational tale of success. The Sovereign story contains lessons for everyone who is in business, whether they be the owners of small businesses or the managers of larger organisations. Sometimes knowingly, and some times just by intuition, Coon and Hendry built an amazingly successful business, and they did so by employing ten basic principles of business management.

1. Create superior customer value.
Business is the activity of creating value. That is what we get paid to do. Customers do not want your products and services; they want what your products and services will do for them. Coon and Hendry understood this, and that is why they knew it would not be enough to deliver good customer service. They knew they had to deliver superior value, both to independent advisers and to policyholders.

Coon got the idea to start Sovereign from seeing that New Zealand's established life offices were offering New Zealanders life products that were low in value by overseas standards. Among other things, they were not customer friendly and they lacked flexibility. Coon believed that if he introduced the more progressive policies that were commonplace in England, customers would recognise the superior value and flock to purchase them. He was right, and from the beginning Sovereign's sales exceeded his forecasts. "We got the products right," says Uganecz. "They were significantly better than the other life companies' products and we provided investors access to an exceptional range of markets anywhere in the world. The flexibility we built into our products meant they never needed to become obsolete."

The same applied to working with advisers. Whereas the traditional companies took their salaried advisers for granted (some would even say they abused them), Sovereign treated them as their primary customers. Being customer driven, rather than just customer focused, they looked at what the advisers needed from Sovereign in order to be successful, and they changed the way Sovereign did things as a result. Later, they lifted their game yet again and treated advisers as business partners, and worked with them to improve not just their sales, but the way they ran their businesses.

The aim at Sovereign has always been not just to service or satisfy their customers, but to make them successful. This has been the goal whether the customers were policyholders needing to protect themselves against risks or to prepare for their retirement, or advisers trying to build successful businesses.

2. Operate efficient processes.

Hendry knew that operational efficiency is essential to being successful in business. Efficiency results in lower costs and also in better service for customers. Ballantyne shared Hendry's view and between them they set Sovereign on a ruthless, never-ending quest for improved efficiency. Both understood that the key to that efficiency was to understand and streamline Sovereign's business processes. "What we learned," says Ballantyne, "was that you have to have systems that will allow you to deliver what you promise. Our approach was to put processes in place from the beginning and then constantly work to improve them." Hendry and Ballantyne made use of the twin tools of TQM and IT to do this.

3. Develop people in teams.

Teamwork has been the foundation block of the Sovereign culture. In the early days, when the company was small, Sovereign was one team. Hendry and Coon were easily accessible to all staff, they worked together doing whatever had to be done to deliver to the customer, and they socialised together. As the company grew, the teamwork process needed to be formalised. Ballantyne led this by organising her operations division into multi-skilled business units, each of which was focused on servicing a particular group of customers. Sovereign's experience has been that teamwork leads to both improved operating efficiency and customer satisfaction. Teamwork also encourages people to take ownership of problems and therefore facilitates empowerment. That in turn encourages multi-skilling and increases job satisfaction. One of Sovereign's most significant achievements in the operations area was to turn employees into business people by organising them into business units and giving them the responsibility of looking after a defined set of customers.

> *"In order to be irreplaceable, one must always be different."*
> Coco Chanel

4. Re-invent your business.

Not only did Coon and Hendry re-invent the life assurance industry, they continued to re-invent Sovereign throughout its 12 year history. Products were continuously re-developed and product launches, such as the simulcast, were usually New Zealand firsts. The Underwriter's Guide and Healthscreen revolutionised the way policies were issued. Sovereign has spent a great deal of money over the years developing computer systems, such as Aegis and Platform Z that were world leaders in the insurance industry. Some innovations, such as NZ Superannuation Services, have not been so successful, but Hendry would be the first to claim that if you are not making mistakes, you are not pushing the boundaries hard enough. "We worked hard at being entrepreneurial and innovative," says Ballantyne. "Even when we became a large company."

5. Develop a business strategy.

There is a difference between having a business strategy and managing a business to optimise its performance. Having operational effectiveness means you are running the same race faster than your competitors. Having a business strategy, on the other hand, is choosing to run a different race, a race that you believe you can win because of some competitive advantage that you have. Successful entrepreneurs position themselves differently by studying the market and finding needs that existing companies are not catering for, and then they set out to develop products and services that will satisfy those unmet needs. This is clearly what Coon did. His strategy excited all who heard it and caused the traditional life companies in New Zealand to spend years trying to play catch up, a difficult task given that Coon and Hendry had stacked the race to suit their strengths. Sovereign therefore had a healthy head start by the time their competitors were reacting. This point of difference was carried through to every part of Sovereign, including marketing the company. "In text, graphic treatment, advertising and other areas of physical evidence, we consciously differed from the norm and from expectations. In the end, the competition were forced to follow," says Whitney.

> *"If you can dream it, you can do it. Always remember this whole thing was started by a mouse."*
> Walt Disney

6. Be an effective leader.

Experience has shown that the most successful entrepreneurs are those who are effective leaders as well as competent managers. Effective leaders share five characteristics, and the first of these is that they have a vision for their company. They know what they want to achieve, but more importantly, because business is the activity of creating value, their vision is of the value their company can create for its customers, their staff and the community around them, as well as for their shareholders. Not only do successful entrepreneurs have this vision, they care passionately about it. It is obvious to anyone who meets them that this vision is something they truly believe and care about. In fact, it dominates their lives. Because of their passion, effective leaders communicate their vision constantly to anyone who will listen. As a result, they attract people who want to work with them, people who are inspired by their vision, their personal conviction and their enthusiasm. So it was with Coon. He is not by nature an extrovert, fond of being the centre of attention. He is most comfortable sitting alone in front of his computer building intricate financial models. But he had a vision that he cared about passionately, and still cares passionately about to this day. The main reason he is remaining as a consultant to Sovereign is that he has spotted an opportunity to introduce some new products into the marketplace. From his first trips to New Zealand, Coon could see a business opportunity, but more importantly, he could see what developing that opportunity could do for his customers, his staff, and his business partners, as well as for himself. He could picture the company that he could build and, most importantly, he could foresee how it would transform the insurance industry and improve the lives of brokers and policyholders. This has been an important part of Sovereign's success. "If you can get people to buy into your vision, you can do anything," says Ballantyne.

Coon and Hendry were passionate about Sovereign as being something more than just a company. They both had very high expectations of Sovereign from the start. "In all my work experience I have never seen such fervour in how they feel about Sovereign, how they live and breathe making Sovereign continue to make a difference in peoples' lives, and how protective they are of the Sovereign name and experience," says Whitney. The challenge has always been that when the company expanded, those filling the positions did not necessarily have the same level of passion, commitment or understanding. This is the major challenge facing Sovereign today, as it tries to assimilate the Colonial people and move forward under new leadership.

7. Develop strategic alliances.

Commerce is a social activity and, therefore, it is not possible to succeed in business by working on your own. Coon and Hendry knew this, and they also understood that the more strategic alliances they could develop, the easier it would be to launch their new life company. Coon's arrangements with some of the world's leading reassurers gave Sovereign an on-going source of funding, and the partnership they formalised with Eagle Star gave the fledgling company credibility. This was also true of their association with some of the world's top fund managers. Kay Coyne's contacts helped Sovereign defend itself against accusations from the Securities Commission, and David Belcher's contact with Ralph Norris helped Coon and Hendry sell Sovereign to the ASB Bank. If that was the case for Sovereign, it will be the same for you and your business. Who can help you to achieve your goals? Who would benefit from helping you to reach your goals? Look for synergies and win-win situations. Work to find suitable associates and partners, and build and maintain relationships with them. Do not be afraid to give up something. Owning 70% of something is a lot better than owning 100% of nothing.

8. Hire the right people, support them and reward them.

Herb Kellagher, the owner of Southwest Airlines, one of the most successful airlines in the world, advises business leaders to hire for attitude and train for skill. Kellagher suggests managers should hire people who share their vision and their values; give them support and opportunities to learn and then let them have the freedom to use their expertise to grow the business. This has always been Coon and Hendry's view. From the beginning, they were less interested in the skills and experience of their prospective employees than in their attitude towards the Sovereign dream. Ballantyne is a good case in point. Coon and Hendry were happy to employ her in spite of her youth and relatively little experience in the life industry because of her attitude towards the established companies and her excitement about what they were trying to accomplish at Sovereign. From the moment she came on board she was given freedom and responsibility, and this grew as she demonstrated her ability. Over the years they gave her numerous opportunities to develop her abilities further. They also gave her their unwavering support. This was the way Ballantyne managed her people, too. "My philosophy has always been to give people their heads. I let them know the intent of the business, treated them well and then let them get on with it," she says.

Getting on with it does not mean leaving people to flounder, however. Sovereign has always ensured that people were giving the supervision, training and tools they needed to succeed in their jobs. "When you were promoted to the team leader position," says Lyn Dorreen, "the support network was there. You could ask to go on courses and you would get quarterly reviews. These involved discussions about past goals and whether they had been met, and also setting new goals. These sessions really helped me to focus on what I wanted to get out of my job, and also helped me to work better with my staff."

Once they joined the Sovereign family, staff were always well looked after. Sovereign is a generous employer, not just in salary paid, but in other benefits, such as support for staff social activities. For example, Sovereign always celebrates Christmas in style. It is a black tie affair staged at places such as Kellihers on Puketutu Island, the Auckland Town Hall or The Carlton. Invitations are custom designed. A lot of effort is also put into staging Christmas parties for the children of Sovereign staff. Staff sports teams get company sponsorship and a lot of effort goes into helping staff to keep fit and healthy.

9. Set high standards.

Anyone working for Coon and Hendry, be they employees or suppliers, quickly understood that they had very high standards, and they expected these would be met consistently. They had very high expectations of themselves, too, and they expected no more from others than they expected from themselves. Hendry, in particular, would make it very clear to people when he was not happy with someone's performance. Suppliers who did not meet his expectations found they were not doing business with Sovereign for very long, and employees who had trouble living up to these standards usually made the decision to work elsewhere.

Ballantyne's work with TQM put a hard edge to these expectations. Standards of performance were formalised, and systems and key performance indicators were put in place to measure performance in real time. If those standards were not met, work was done to improve the processes and systems that were letting the company and its customers down.

"If you want to be a great company, you have to start acting like one today."

Thomas J Watson, founder of IBM

10. Think big, look big, act big.

"You must always be seen as a company that excels in marketing," says Ballantyne. "You have to radiate confidence and appear to be bigger than you are." Hendry always had a long-term view of what he wanted to achieve in the marketing area. He had, even for a small company, big ideas, and he also had the talent and determination to reach them. "In the initial stages of Sovereign he kept us, in all situations, focused on where we were going as opposed to where we were," says Whitney. "We were planning-driven versus having a particular tactical bias, such as to get the ads on TV quickly." Hendry was also very good at making a little go a long way. Budgetary constraints were a very real issue from the outset, and they have continued to be important over the years, but that has not stopped Sovereign from spending money on key events that made the company look bigger than it was. The sponsorship of the Newstalk 1ZB business programme and the use of signage around sports fields are examples of how relatively small investments had a big impact.

In addition to these ten business principles, Coon and Hendry have followed five personal success strategies.

1. Get experience.

Douglas Myers, former CEO and chairman of Lion Nathan, and arguably one of New Zealand's most successful business leaders, urges would-be entrepreneurs to get relevant work experience in someone else's business before launching their own. That is just what Coon and Hendry did.

By the time Coon and Hendry came to New Zealand, each had spent decades learning the life business. Nothing they would need to do to establish an insurance company in New Zealand was new to them. Coon had spent several years developing insurance products that were customer-focused, flexible and user-friendly. He had negotiated financial arrangements with reassurers that were unknown in New Zealand, and he had developed valuable contacts with some of the most experienced and senior players in the industry. Hendry had learned how to run an insurance company from the bottom up and had spent the last six years building a life insurance company from scratch in Hong Kong. He was experienced in marketing and sales, a competent systems person and a good people manager. Former Chairman Dennis Ferrier did a thorough check of Coon and Hendry before agreeing to join the Sovereign Board. Said Ferrier, "they have been recommended to me, and have turned out to be two of the most talented and genuinely nice people I have had the pleasure of working with." Coon and Hendry understood the life assurance business, they knew what had to be done to succeed. After all, they had done it before.

"Whether you think you can or you think you can't, you are right."
Henry Ford

2. Believe in yourself.

Like most successful entrepreneurs, Coon and Hendry had a blind belief in their invulnerability. In the early days, it just never occurred to them that they might fail. They simply forged ahead with single-mindedness and conviction. Their confidence has been infectious and Sovereign's managers have had confidence in their own abilities from the outset. This was made easier because everyone involved in Sovereign had a clear belief about the benefits their products and services would bring to a market lacking real competition. Coon and Hendry were also on a mission they believed in. They were determined to take an upstart company and build it into New Zealand's premier financial services group.

3. Take the risk.

Coon and Hendry understood that business is a four-letter word spelled R I S K. They knew that, at the end of the day, if their vision was going to become reality, they would have to take significant risks, both personally and on behalf of the company. They were prepared to leave their comfortable jobs, move to a new country and put their assets on the line. They were also prepared to expose themselves to criticism, attack and failure. Over the years, Coon and Hendry have made some very tough decisions with resolution. They have been able to do this because they have never been afraid of making mistakes. "We knew we had to run quickly, take risks and be determined to succeed," says Ballantyne. "Ian has always said that he would rather make the wrong decision than make no decision at all." When it became clear that a mistake had been made, Coon and Hendry had no problems owning up to it, and then acting decisively to put things right. Both have the ability to get to the root of the problem, define a solution, and put this into action.

4. Persevere.

To succeed in business, as in all activities, there has never been a substitute for hard work. But perseverance is even more important. The test of your character is not what you do on your first and second attempt but how you perform on the fifth and sixth attempt. Success does not come easily or quickly. It comes to those who persevere. There are many occasions when it would have been easier for Coon and Hendry to give up. In the early days, the knock-backs from brokers were constant. Then there were the problems with the Securities Commission. Next, Eagle Star, their so-called friend, tried to steal the company from them. Later, the public listing tested them. It took two attempts before the company successfully listed on the New Zealand stock exchange and then when it did, its share price languished. Instead of giving up and accepting that Sovereign would have to try to survive without the capital it needed, Coon and Hendry worked to find a purchaser who would provide them with the capital they needed but allow them to continue running the business independently.

5. Have clear values.

From the beginning, the staff at Sovereign knew that they should do the right thing. Right, to Coon and Hendry, always meant acting with honesty and integrity. This was not merely a view they developed as a business strategy, it is the philosophy they each live by. They were very successful in getting this message across to their staff, and the core values of Sovereign were understood by all: to be world leaders, to do the right thing, and to look after people. "Right from the beginning, we all wanted to do the same thing," says Lyn Dorreen. "We wanted to be honest and we wanted to do the right thing for the customer. We were very customer focused. Even now we teach new people that this is what it is all about."

Coon and Hendry have also placed a premium on loyalty. Those who supported Sovereign from the start have earned a special position of recognition. Coon and Hendry stand behind people who work for and with them. Most importantly, they have worked hard to make sure that everyone in Sovereign understands that these are the core values that should guide their behaviour. The message has got through. "You have to be clear about what is right and what is wrong," says Ballantyne, "and then take corrective action when it is wrong."

Ten basic business principles, five personal strategies and two courageous and determined men with a vision, lie behind the remarkable success of Sovereign. Coon and Hendry would be the first to tell you that they could not always have articulated these principles. They were part of the 'golden guts', the intuition by which they ran Sovereign. This is where you have an advantage they did not have. You can benefit from their experience. You can use these principles as a blueprint for how you run your business. After all, the Sovereign story shows they work. They worked for Coon and Hendry and they can work for you. All you have to do is do it.

As the old saying goes, "If it's going to be, it's up to me."

About The Authors

Dr. Ian Brooks

Dr Ian Brooks has written eight books, many of which are best-sellers, on business management and customer care. His books have sold a total of over 40,000 copies in New Zealand alone. This makes him the most published author in business management in New Zealand's history. His most recent books, both published in 2001, are *10 Steps to Becoming Customer Driven* and *The Businessperson's Toolbox of Really Useful Ideas*. He is currently writing a book on pricing, called *Persuade Your Customers to Pay More*, which will be available in March, 2002.

A much sought after and internationally recognised business speaker, Ian inspires and entertains over 180 audiences each year in New Zealand, Canada, the United States, Great Britain and Australia. He is one of only six New Zealanders to speak at the *Million Dollar Round Table* in America, the world's largest convention of insurance agents.

Ian is one of New Zealand's foremost business advisers. For nearly 25 years, he has consulted to organisations in New Zealand, Australia, Canada and the South Pacific helping them to survive and grow in this crowded and competitive market place. Ian's clients have included large corporations, such as CSR, Air New Zealand, Telecom, WestpacTrust, Carter Holt Harvey and Fletcher Challenge, and many small and medium sized businesses. Ian also has experience in the public sector, having consulted to Canada Customs, and a large number of local bodies including the Auckland, Dunedin and Hamilton City Councils. Ian is recognised for his expertise in customer care, organisational change, human resource management, quality management, and business strategy.

You can hear Ian talk about creating customer value and customer relationship management, watch him explain how to turn complaints into cash, see him discuss how to become customer driven, download outlines of his speeches and obtain more information about Ian by visiting **www.ianbrooks.com**

To contact Ian, email ian@ianbrooks.com

Dwight Whitney

Born in the United States and now living in New Zealand, Dwight is an experienced communicator and marketer with over 27 years experience. For over 10 years, he and his partner, Kaye Coyne, were Sovereign's marketing consultants.

During his career, Dwight has held a number of other marketing and communications positions in business, including being a writer for the international marketing division of Japan Broadcasting Corporation (NHK) in Japan; a staff writer and editor of Metro Magazine and marketing manager for the Strathmore Group.

Since 1986 Dwight has worked as a communication consultant, both in his own business and as a senior consultant for DDB Pinnacle. His experience spans a number of industry sectors including financial services, professional services, exporting, education, and energy and utility management. He also has experience in industries such as publishing, aviation, sports, tourism, news media and entertainment, logistics management, agribusiness and information technology.

Dwight has a Bachelor of Arts from the University of Auckland, a Masters in Communication from the University of Hawaii and a Diploma in Communication Policy and Planning from the East-West Centre in Honolulu. He has taught graduate courses in public relations and communication at Unitec and has lectured at AUT and an international United Nations symposium on communication.